"The apostle Paul summarised his ministry experience as combined agony and ecstasy: 'death is at work in us, but life in you.' Matt Fuller well captures this paradoxical balance. A modern-day Barnabas, he writes encouragingly but honestly, coupling the hard-earned wisdom of personal experience with the field-tested insights of past masters. *The Joyful Pastor* is a gift to pastors, present and future—as well as to the pastored."

SINCLAIR FERGUSON, Teaching Fellow, Ligonier Ministries; Author, *The Whole Christ*

"Written from the trenches, not the bleachers, *The Joyful Pastor* is a theologically rich, pastorally honest call to recover what we too easily lose: the breathtaking privilege of shepherding souls purchased by Christ's own blood. Fuller doesn't deny the sorrows. He simply refuses to let them have the last word. Every weary pastor needs this book. You will be glad you've read it."

JUAN SANCHEZ, Senior Pastor, High Pointe Baptist Church, Austin, TX

"The realities of pastoral ministry are learned not in the classroom but in the trenches of the local church. Pastors reading this book will identify with so much that Matt describes and be encouraged to keep going, understanding that there really is no greater task."

JONATHAN PRIME, FIEC Director for London

"Every pastor—discouraged or not—should read this. It is jam-packed with scriptural truth, personal pastoral experience and rich quotations from church history. An encouraging, practical, thoughtful and pastorally careful read!"

ANDY MASON, Mission Director, Co-Mission; Vicar, St John's Chelsea, London; Author, *God's Leader*

"This book may be written for church pastors but it is equally relevant for women and men involved in a variety of word ministries, Matt reminds us that ministry is a noble task, full of joys and sorrows, but that even the darkest of times can be used by the Lord to mould us into his likeness and thwart Satan's scheming. Here is pastoral wisdom resulting from years of faithful ministry. It warmed my heart to read it."

CARRIE SANDOM, Director of Women's Ministry, Proclamation Trust, London

"As pastors, we sometimes use the line 'I have the best job in the world!' I worry that sometimes we give the impression that it's one of the very worst. Perhaps we sometimes believe it is. Matt's book is a wonderful balm for anyone feeling the wear and tear of ministry. I am thankful to have read it. It's done my soul and my ministry a power of good."

RORY SHINER, Senior Pastor, Providence City Church, Perth, Australia; Author, *The World Next Door*

"This is an unusual and beautiful book. It is semi-autobiographical, which is unusual for a Christian book. It is beautiful because it describes the life of a real pastor not at the end of their ministry but in the midst of it, finding joy to keep going. I will be encouraging the next generation of pastors, as well as those of my own generation, to read it."

ROBIN SYDSERFF, Director, The Proclamation Trust, UK

"I wish I had had this book in the early days of my ministry. Matt is honest about the frustrations and challenges of ministry but shows how they are far outweighed by the privileges and delights of knowing and serving Christ. Biblically faithful and pastorally warm—highly recommended."

PAUL MALLARD, Chair, FIEC Theology Team, UK; former Pastor, Widcombe Baptist Church, Bath

"Here is a timely tonic for the pastor's soul. The job is tough, and discouragements press in. What a help to be reminded of the many privileges of the role and to be called afresh to rejoice in the Lord. This book is at once theological and pastoral, and it manages to be honest, realistic and optimistic all the while. I want every pastor I know to read it."

JONATHAN GRIFFITHS, President, Heritage College and Seminary, Ontario, Canada; Bible Teacher, Encounter the Truth

"A deeply encouraging and refreshingly honest book for weary shepherds. Drawing from decades of pastoral experience, Matt Fuller combines rich biblical insight, wise pastoral application, and the steady counsel of the Puritans and other faithful voices from church history to remind ministers of the privilege and joy of shepherding God's people. It strengthens both the heart and the hands of pastors for long-term ministry."

TONY MERIDA, Pastor, Imago Dei Church, Raleigh, NC; Author, *Love Your Church*

"*The Joyful Pastor* is like dinner with a dear friend—full of honesty, winsome discussion, deep encouragement and rich sustenance. But Matt Fuller has served gospel ministers by inviting us to dine not just with him but with those from centuries past who have served the same Lord. A must-read for anyone in ministry—and not just once but, I would suggest, annually."

PAUL GRIMMOND, Vice-Principal, Moore College, Sydney

Matt Fuller

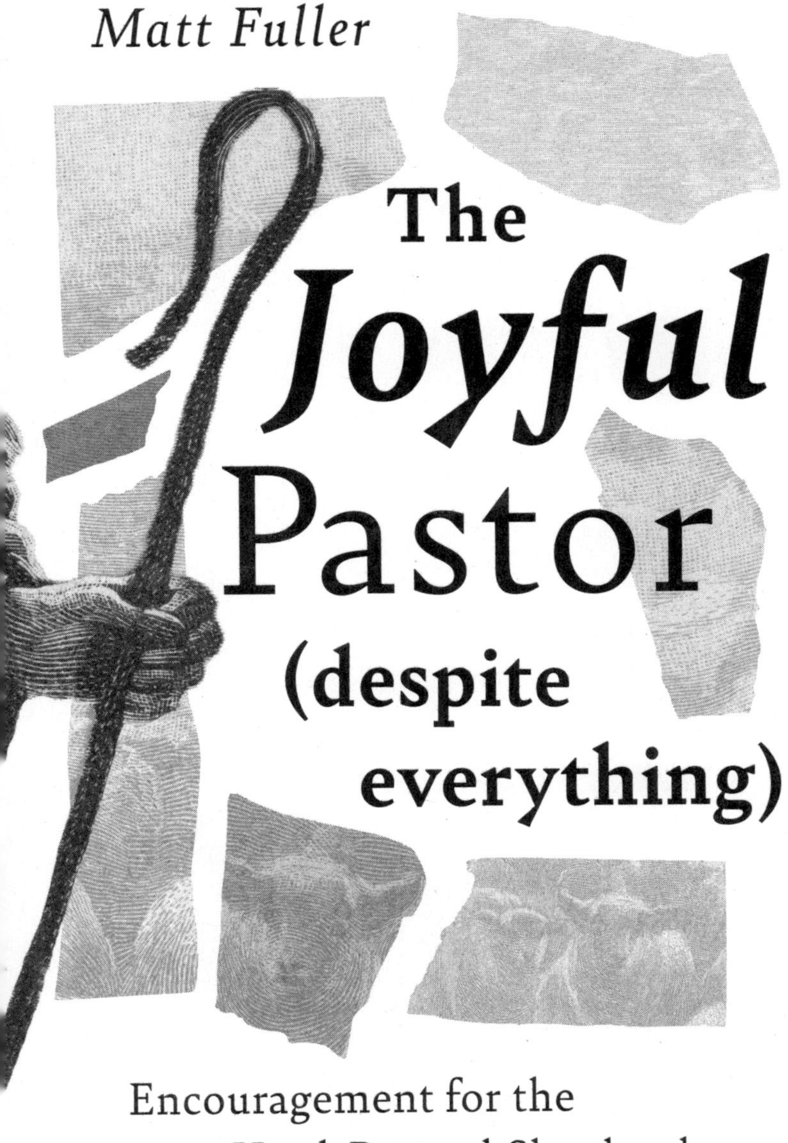

The *Joyful* Pastor (despite everything)

Encouragement for the Hard-Pressed Shepherd

thegoodbook COMPANY

The Joyful Pastor

Published by:
The Good Book Company

thegoodbook.com | thegoodbook.co.uk
thegoodbook.com.au | thegoodbook.co.nz

Titles published by The Good Book Company may be purchased in bulk for educational, business, fundraising or sales promotional use. For information and bespoke pricing, please email SpecialMarkets@thegoodbook.com.

All emphases in Scripture quotations are the author's.

Every book published by The Good Book Company has been written by a human author and edited by a human editor. While AI tools are sometimes used to assist with research and support certain processes, all content has been created by a human author and thoroughly checked by our editorial team to ensure it is biblically faithful and pastorally wise.

Cover design by Drew McCall

ISBN: 9781802544329 | JOB-008877 | Printed in India

Dedicated to the many staff at Christ Church who have shared the joys and sorrows of ministry over 25 years, especially Sharon, Ben and Phil, for decades of encouragement amid the chaos.

Contents

Chapter 1

A Sorrow Full of Joy

Before I went into ministry, I was a schoolteacher. I loved the job. I would happily have spent 40 years as a schoolteacher.

But one thing that I observed as a teacher was that a number of staff in their fifties had run out of steam. Not all, by any stretch—but quite a few were seeing out their time and, in the case of a couple of maths teachers, quite literally counting down the days until they retired. After years in the profession, they were tired, they were discouraged and, in some cases, they were bored. Consequently, the kids they taught were bored because there was no enthusiasm in the classroom; their teacher was just going through the motions.

With the reckless and naïve enthusiasm of a 20-something-year-old, I promised myself that I would never allow myself to feel that way.

Now I'm in my fifties, and after 25 years of ministry, I often think back to that experience. I'm certainly not bored, but sometimes I do feel tired or discouraged, or both. There are certainly times when I don't seem to quite have the same energy levels as before. The early zeal and sense of expectancy in ministry can sometimes be buried by the sorrows and sadnesses. It's easier to focus on what's going wrong than to notice what has gone well.

To clarify, I remain 100% convinced that ministry is "a noble task", as Paul put it (1 Timothy 3:1). At one stage I had thought of that as the title for this book. When I've been at my lowest ebb, I have never doubted that. I always still believed that ministry was an excellent thing to do—a noble thing to do; but I was in danger of losing my zeal and wanting others to do it instead of me. I can see in myself how easy it is to become the pastor version of those older teachers I was so sure I would not follow.

I want—need—to remind myself of the *joys and privileges* of being in pastoral ministry. I want to recover my enthusiasm and maintain my spiritual fervour. I want to be a shepherd as described by Peter, doing it "not because you must, but because you are willing, as God wants you to be ... eager to serve" (1 Peter 5:2). I want to be able to say with Matthew Scott, a 19th-century English minister...

> With all my discouragements and sinful despondency, in my better moments, I can think of no work worth doing compared to this. If I had a thousand lives, I would willingly spend them in it: and if I had as many sons, I would gladly [encourage them into it].[1]

---

1 Matthew Scott, quoted in Charles Bridges, *The Christian Ministry* (Pantianos Classics, 1831), p. 19.

I don't want to be a discouraged, somewhat grumpy pastor. I want to be a willing and eager pastor. A joyful pastor.

(By the way, throughout this book I'm going to use "pastors" as my primary shorthand for those in ministry: men and women, senior ministers, associates and juniors. The pressures and demands, joys and opportunities are not all the same for these different roles, but there's plenty of common ground. If you're in full-time church ministry and are not a "pastor", this book is still for you, and I hope that you'll forgive my shorthand.)

The Stories We Tell

I love one of John Newton's lesser-known hymns, "What Contradictions Meet", in which he beautifully describes the strange mixture of emotions in the life of a pastor:

> What contradictions meet
> In ministers' employ!
> It is a bitter sweet—
> A sorrow full of joy
> No other post affords a place
> For equal honour or disgrace.[2]

It has a wonderful realism to it: in ministry there is both bitterness and sweetness, sorrow and joy. But my theory is that lots of us pastors are well aware of the sorrows of ministry: we quickly notice them; we dwell on them; we dream about them. The joys? Less so.

---

2 https://hymnary.org/text/what_contradictions_meet (accessed 2 March 2026).

How Not to Be "Quite Miserable"

Last year I began visiting an elderly retired minister who lives near me. He's now fairly chairbound but delights in having visitors. The first time I went to see him, he asked what was going on in the ministry at Christ Church Mayfair, how long I had been there, and what I had seen the Lord doing. So I painted a brief portrait of the last few years, and his response arrested me:

> Brother, you must be overflowing with thankfulness.

My response was along the lines of...

> Hmm, I'm afraid I'm not. Most of the time I'm stumbling through from one week to the next, worried about some crisis or other.

He replied...

> No, no. That's no good. Brother, you must pause and give thanks. You'll be quite miserable otherwise.

I found that a profoundly helpful word. And I have sought to do as he counselled.

My resolution to give thanks more frequently has been helped by the fact that while this elderly man still has a sparkling wit, his short-term memory is a little shot. So now, when I visit him every few weeks, I quite often relay the same stories I have already told him. He consistently comments, "Brother, you must be overflowing with thankfulness".

And now I'm prepared and can reply, "I'm learning to".

I don't think thankfulness is my natural setting, and

I'm not yet overflowing, but gratitude does now trickle out of me.

What are the stories you tell yourself about your ministry, and what are the stories you share with other pastors? It's often easier to notice, dwell upon and talk about the sorrows than the joys. Bad news often comes as a sudden event, while good news often happens over a long period of time. The man or woman who is exposed as having an affair and leaves their family is a wildly discouraging event that looms large. By contrast, the believer who slowly grows in maturity as a Christian, who joined your church when they weren't a believer but ten years later is now leading Bible studies, evangelising in their neighbourhood and mentoring younger believers is very encouraging. You have to make an effort to focus on the slow-burn success stories.

Years ago, I remember asking Peter Horrocks, who was then head of BBC News, why they had spent days and days covering an English sporting victory as headline news.[3] His words stuck in my head: "Most news events are depressing. Most of the time it's war, famine, disaster, political failure. Good news stories tend to take years to happen, and no one has the attention span. So when a good news event comes along, you have to squeeze every bit of joy from it."

Most churches will have some people in them who are quietly bearing fruit 30, 60 or 100-fold. As pastors, as we consider our ministry we need to deliberately

---

3 I want to tell you that this was England regaining the Ashes trophy by beating Australia at cricket in 2005 after 18 long years. I include this detail here just for Australian friends. I am also aware that 2005 is now a long time ago...

take time to notice these good news stories, to squeeze every drop of joy from the things that go well. I say this as one whose temperament is not naturally positive. Thankfulness is a discipline for me; I have to remember to do it. I have made it my habit to write down five things I'm thankful for in the past 24 hours. Similarly, in our weekly meetings as a staff team I insist that everyone has to share at least one encouragement from the previous week. We try to celebrate encouragements publicly at church. I constantly find it amazing how many petitions that we've prayed at church prayer meetings have been answered. It's encouraging!

It's not only within our own hearts and churches—we pastors can probably also be better at encouraging one another. It may be a British thing, but when we meet up, lots of ministers don't want to be perceived as boasting and don't want to discourage others who are in tricky seasons, so we don't list out the things we're thankful for. We don't give thanks to God for seeing him at work. We share everything that is going wrong and can easily lament over the things that are discouraging.

Perhaps we need to speak as much about the joys as we do the sorrows—as much about the sweetness as the bitterness. Newton's hymn is worth reading in full because it has a lovely balance to it:

> What contradictions meet
> In ministers' employ!
> It is a bitter sweet--
> A sorrow full of joy;
> No other post affords a place
> For equal honour or disgrace!

Who can describe the pain
Which faithful preachers feel,
Constrain'd to preach in vain
To hearts as hard as steel?
Or who can tell the pleasures felt
When stubborn hearts begin to melt?

The Saviour's dying love,
The soul's amazing worth,
Their utmost efforts move
And draw their bowels forth:
They pray and strive--their rest departs
Till Christ be form'd in sinners hearts.

If some small hope appear,
They still are not content,
But with a jealous fear,
They watch for the event:
Too oft they find their hopes deceiv'd;
Then how their inmost souls are griev'd!

But when their pains succeed,
And from the tender blade
The rip'ning ears proceed,
Their toils are overpaid:
No harvest-joy can equal theirs,
To find the fruit of all their cares.

On what has now been sown,
Thy blessing, Lord bestow;
The power is thine alone
To make it spring and grow;
Do thou the gracious harvest raise,
And thou, alone, shalt have the praise.

So, in order redress the balance a little, this book is going to focus on the joys and somewhat take the sorrows for granted. I'm not attempting to be balanced. This is meant to be a lopsided book! I want to spend the majority of the time dwelling upon the blessings and privileges of pastoral ministry.

At this point, another clarification feels in order. I have not reached some new level of ministry joyfulness and bliss. I'm not writing this from the beach while having happy daydreams because all is well. I'm writing amid chaos. On my desk are significant staffing issues, a domestic abuse case in marriage, a suicide attempt, a financial shortfall in the budget and a lack of leaders for various ministries. There are numerous issues at church that have rumbled on for years and seem intractable. I have had numerous critics in our church. As a family, we are waiting for a sibling to die of terminal illness, and we are worried about elderly parents. I certainly feel "hard pressed". In part, I am writing this to remind myself of why I am "not crushed" (2 Corinthians 4:8). In truth, I wonder if I'm writing this in part as a form of task avoidance. However, chiefly, I'm trying to pause and give thanks.

If I were the only minister in Christendom who feels like this, then I'd be thrilled. I would still write this book for myself; I need it. But I don't think I'm alone. I'm conscious that many of my peers in the UK feel a little jaded, and when I've told friends, especially in the USA and Australia, that I was planning to write this, they replied, "Yes please". The data that's available suggests that, worse than feeling jaded, somewhere around a third of pastors consider quitting at some point each year.[4] Often there are tragic stories behind some of that. Yet I wonder if, for many of us, there is no great drama; rather it's an attritional sense of becoming wearied, an anxiety over the fact that the finishing line is a long way off.

Of course, it's not only in their fifties that people start to wonder about their life choices! In one of his less encouraging passages, the 19th-century minister Charles Bridges observed:

> A distant view of the ministry is generally very different from what is found when we are actually engaged in it. The young soldier, who has never seen an enemy, may form some general notions of what is before him; but his ideas will be much more lively and diversified when he comes upon the field of battle. If the Lord were to show us the whole beforehand, who that has a sense of his own insufficiency and weakness would venture to engage?[5]

It's a typically robust sentence from Bridges, but you may only be a few years into ministry and yet know the

---

4 It is hard to get accurate data here. Some of the articles I found with relevant information were the following (all accessed 2 March 2026):
https://apnews.com/article/christian-clergy-burnout-pandemic-survey-24ee46327438ff46b074d234ffe2f58c
https://apnews.com/article/clergy-burnout-church-mental-health-summit-570e71ec96575abc92865ad5baf491e6
https://www.christianitytoday.com/2021/11/pastor-burnout-pandemic-barna-consider-leaving-ministry/
https://www.christianitytoday.com/2015/09/one-percent-why-so-few-evangelical-pastors-quit-lifeway/
https://www.ministrybrands.com/church-management/ministry-burnout

5 Charles Bridges, *The Christian Ministry,* p. 105.

reality of what he is saying. When we enter ministry, it tends to turn out to be a lot more complicated than we thought before we started! Perhaps three years into ministry (or sooner), you have discovered that there are days when it's no fun and very different than you'd imagined it would be.

Perhaps you aren't yet several years in, though—perhaps you are reading this just as you enter ministry. Don't panic. It turns out that a sense of our own insufficiency and weakness can put us in a very healthy place spiritually.

As I've turned to previous generations of minsters (which we'll do throughout this book), I have been struck by the fact that there is nothing new here. For pastors, the temptation towards discouragement is always there. Two hundred years ago, Bridges wrote:

> Unless we have a high estimate of the church; the constraining influence of the Saviour's love, and the upholding prop of almighty grace, what is there to preserve us from sinking in despondency?[6]

Despondency is often a close companion to those in ministry. Paul could write that "we were under great pressure, far beyond our ability to endure, so that we despaired of life itself" (2 Corinthians 1:8). We need to take our time to raise our view of the church, the Saviour's love and the prop of almighty grace. We need to fight the natural drift towards sin and despondency. Although Bridges doesn't make the link here, it is often despondency that opens a door in our hearts for sin.

6 As above, p. 12.

All of a sudden, in our self-pity, we can begin to feel entitled to indulge unhealthy patterns of behaviour.

Instead of this, we need to hear the New Testament command to "rejoice in the Lord always. I will say it again, rejoice" (Philippians 4:4). We need to heed the command to "never be lacking in zeal, but keep your spiritual fervour, serving the Lord" (Romans 12:11). It's clearly very easy to stop rejoicing and to lose zeal! But we also need to remember why we can rejoice—why we can get up with a sense of zeal for what we are doing. We need to pause and give thanks so that we don't end up "quite miserable".

The Best Vocation in the World

Centuries ago, the Puritan Thomas Goodwin observed:

> The work of the ministry is the best work in the world; God had but one Son in the world and he made him a minister.[7]

I want to recover the sense that I have the best job in the world. No one enters full-time ministry for the "big bucks" (or, at least, they shouldn't). No one does it for an easy life. We entered ministry because we felt it was a vocation, not merely a job. Most of us presumably felt that nothing was more important than serving Jesus by preaching, teaching and shepherding, and taking out the message of the gospel. Here was a task that gave purpose to our lives.

---

7 Thomas Goodwin, "An Exposition of the First Chapter of the Epistle to the Ephesians" in *The Works of Thomas Goodwin* (Reformation Heritage Books, 2006), 1:563.

Brothers and sisters, that remains true. Consider Richard Baxter's 17th-century description of the pastor's task:

> We are seeking to uphold the world, to save it from the curse of God, to perfect the creation, to attain the ends of Christ's death, to save ourselves and others from damnation, to overcome the devil and demolish his kingdom, to set up the kingdom of Christ, and to attain and help others to the kingdom of glory.[8]

That sounds good! The next time that someone asks me what I "do for work", I'm going to try and trot that out. It is true—we are not involved in trifling work that doesn't matter. We are about eternal work that transforms lives.

Think for a moment about writing your resumé. (I've avoided the need to do that by being in the same church for 25 years.) What an extraordinary job description every church pastor has:

- We are shepherds of God's flock (1 Peter 5:1-2).
- We are stewards of God's household (Luke 12:43).
- We are watchmen of God's city (Ezekiel 33:7).
- We are labourers in God's field (1 Corinthians 3:6).
- We are builders of God's house (1 Corinthians 3:10).

---

8 Richard Baxter, *The Reformed Pastor* ((Banner of Truth, 1999 reprint), p. 112.

- We are ambassadors with God's message (2 Corinthians 5:20).

The obvious thing that these all have in common is that we are serving the living God by caring for his precious church, which he bought with his own blood. Have we lost the extraordinary, momentous dignity of that role?

I have a good friend who for a few years was a direct report to a US President. It was a demanding job. He would say that even though at the time he was aware of the honour, it is only with hindsight that he can appreciate with absolute wonder the privilege he had. To paraphrase him, "I had direct access to the most powerful man in the world, some of the most confidential information in the world and a budget of billions of dollars. Who on earth thought little me was worthy of that?!"

Those of us in ministry have the same access to God as every believer, but we have also been given time that we can set apart to study the most precious truths in the world and care for the most precious asset that the Almighty has on this planet: his people. Who on earth thought that you and I were worthy of that?!

Perhaps you need to pinch yourself and stand in awe at the privilege of being an ambassador of the Almighty. You may lack a luxury embassy; you may lack a large budget; you may lack a staff team to assist you. But... the one you represent is the incomparable King of kings and Lord of lords, who alone is immortal and who lives in unapproachable light. There is no doubt whatsoever that he will vindicate and reward his ambassadors with absurd generosity and disproportionate munificence.

So the aim in this book is simply to slow down and appreciate the privilege and joys of pastoring. We'll do that mainly by concentrating on this short passage from 1 Peter 5:

> To the elders among you, I appeal as a fellow elder and a witness of Christ's sufferings who also will share in the glory to be revealed: be shepherds of God's flock that is under your care, watching over them—not because you must, but because you are willing, as God wants you to be; not pursuing dishonest gain, but eager to serve; not lording it over those entrusted to you, but being examples to the flock. And when the Chief Shepherd appears, you will receive the crown of glory that will never fade away.
>
> (v 1-4)

I want to address my own heart so that I am, once again, both willing and eager to serve. I'd love you to join me. Brothers and sisters, we have the best job in the world. It has its sorrows, yes—but also, despite everything, many, *many* joys.

Chapter 2

Shepherds for the Great Shepherd

"Unless we have a high estimate of the church, the constraining influence of the Saviour's love and the upholding power of almighty grace, what is there to preserve us from sinking in despondency?"[9]

Let's think about rightly estimating the church of God—the people whom he has bought with his own blood (Acts 20:28).

I once spoke to a Christian who was a soldier and had served with the British Army in Afghanistan during the conflict there in the first decades of this century. He had served on two tours. The first was relatively quiet; the second he described as "lively". He told me about one occasion when he was caught in a firefight against Taliban soldiers on the side of a mountain.

There was a flock of sheep caught in the crossfire.

9 Charles Bridges, *The Christian Ministry*, p. 12. I'm repeating this quote because I am so struck by it.

As bullets smacked into rocks near this soldier so that little fragments of shrapnel and rock were falling on him, he watched a local Afghan shepherd ignore the bullets flying in two directions, walk over to the flock, spread out his arms and call the sheep to him. The sheep clearly knew their master and responded to his voice, and he led them away from the skirmish and into safety. The soldier had a brief moment when he paused and thought, "That was nuts!" and then he returned to the conflict at hand.

He said that it was only later that night, as he lay on his bed reflecting on the day, that he made the obvious Christian connection: the nameless shepherd that day had shown quite exceptional bravery and care for his flock. He was a *man* willing to die for *smelly sheep*. The soldier smiled and said to me, "I have a shepherd far greater: not merely willing to *risk* his life by entering danger but determined to *give* his life, entering death".

What a shepherd!

We have the privilege of following this shepherd and of being his under-shepherds, caring for his flock.

It's the dominant metaphor of our text in 1 Peter 5:

> To the elders among you, I appeal as a fellow elder and a witness of Christ's sufferings who also will share in the glory to be revealed: *be shepherds of God's flock* that is under your care, watching over them—not because you must, but because you are willing, as God wants you to be; not pursuing dishonest gain, but eager to serve; not lording it over those entrusted to you, but being examples to the flock. And when

> the Chief Shepherd appears, you will receive the crown of glory that will never fade away. (v 1-4)

God's Flock

What an extraordinary privilege, that God should put us in charge of his flock. We are to "be shepherds of the church of God, *which he bought with his own blood*" (Acts 20:28). The Lord Jesus gave everything for the church, and now he delegates the care of his most treasured possession to us.

In one of his more famous quotes, Richard Baxter observes:

> Oh, then, let us hear these arguments of Christ, whenever we feel ourselves grow dull and careless: 'Did I die for these souls, and will not you look after them? Were they worth my blood, and are they not worth your labour? Did I come down from heaven to earth, to seek and to save that which was lost; and will you not go to the next door, or street, or village, to seek them? How small is your labour and condescension as to mine! I debased myself to this, but it is your honour to be so employed. Have I done and suffered so much for their salvation, and was I willing to make you a fellow-worker with me, and will you refuse to do that little which lies upon your hands?[10]

While Baxter's tone may be exacting, the truths here are wonderful. If you've read that quote before, slow down

10 Richard Baxter, *The Reformed Pastor*, p. 131.

now and read it again. It is an extraordinary honour to be employed in shepherding the sheep that Christ died for. Earlier in 1 Peter, the apostle reminds his readers that Christians are "a chosen people, a royal priesthood, a holy nation, God's special possession..." in the same way that his Old Testament people were his "treasured possession" (2:9; Exodus 19:5; see Deuteronomy 7:6).

Baxter observes:

> What a high honour it is to be but one of them... But to be the priests of these priests, and the ruler of these kings—this is *such* an honour.[11]

And that, brothers and sisters in ministry, is *our* honour.

Do you have a treasured possession? Most of us might immediately answer in terms of people—a spouse, a child or a parent. That's understandable, although I don't suppose all of them would enjoy being called a "possession". If I have one "thing" that might qualify as a treasured possession, it is my father's watch. My dad was never a wealthy man with any worldly success. He did the same job for over 40 years, selling fuel to farmers in a rural part of the country. But after 40 years' service, in something of a cliché, he was given an expensive watch. He never wore it. He just locked it away in a drawer. After he died, I also kept it locked away, but I have worn it on four occasions: his funeral and those of my mother, his brother and his sister. I intend to wear it again shortly at the wedding of his eldest granddaughter, my niece. I'll wear it at any further weddings of his grandchildren. Otherwise, it

---

11 As above, p. 131 (my emphasis).

remains locked away. Perhaps I am overly sentimental at wanting some representation of him at these events. Maybe I am needlessly cautious about damaging it. Yet it is possibly the only possession that could get damaged or stolen and cause me to be upset. And... *it's just a watch!*

The church is God's treasured possession, and he says to us, *I entrust her to you. There is nothing I care about like her; there is nothing I value like her; there is nothing I would die for like her. And yet, unworthy though you are, I am placing her in your care.*

What an honour!

But God's Flock Can Be Difficult...

So why, when it is such a privilege to be an under-shepherd, do I not always feel that way? Probably because I spend too much time looking at the sheep and not enough at the Chief Shepherd. When I am spending good time with Jesus and seeing the sheep through his eyes, then generally I can feel the honour of my role. When I just look at the sheep, I do not!

I think that's unsurprising; after all, in the Scriptures, calling people "sheep" is a deeply unflattering metaphor. I have always enjoyed John Stott's observation on sheep when he comments on Acts 20:

> Sheep are not at all the clean and cuddly creatures they may appear. In fact, they are dirty, subject to unpleasant pests, and regularly need to be dipped in strong chemicals to rid them of lice, ticks and worms. They are also unintelligent, wayward and obstinate.

> I hesitate to apply the metaphor too closely and characterize the people of God as dirty, lousy or stupid! But some people are a great trial to their pastors (and vice versa).[12]

There's honesty there! And yet still they are the Lord's treasured possession. And no matter how frustrated we may get with sheep who are a trial, I don't suppose too many of us complain out loud the way that Moses did in Numbers 11:

> Moses heard the people of every family wailing at the entrance to their tents. The LORD became exceedingly angry, and Moses was troubled. He asked the LORD, "Why have you brought this trouble on your servant? What have I done to displease you that you put the burden of all these people on me? Did I conceive all these people? Did I give them birth? Why do you tell me to carry them in my arms, as a nurse carries an infant, to the land you promised on oath to their ancestors? Where can I get meat for all these people? They keep wailing to me, 'Give us meat to eat!' I cannot carry all these people by myself; the burden is too heavy for me. If this is how you are going to treat me, please go ahead and kill me—if I have found favour in your eyes—and do not let me face my own ruin." (v 10-15)

That's quite something to say out loud to the Lord: *Why have you burdened me with these people. I can't cope. If this is my ministry, can you just go ahead and*

---

12 John Stott, *The Message of Acts* (IVP UK, 1991), p. 329.

kill me, please? Personally, I've had bad days, and I've occasionally wondered if I should find another career, but I've never said, "If this is my ministry, go ahead and kill me, Lord".

This incident takes place at the marvellously named Kibroth-Hattaavah (graves of craving) as God's people complain about the boring manna (otherwise and more accurately known as God's miraculous provision of food) and look back with distorted memories on the cuisine they enjoyed in Egypt (where they were brutalised slaves who had to make bricks without straw). This is not an accurate or legitimate complaint. We're told that the grumbling began with "the rabble" (v 4) but soon spread throughout the whole community. And isn't that often the way? A small group are disgruntled and manage to drag others into their complaining.

So Moses is forced to deal with an unreasonable and growing complaint against his leadership. He is a model of an unhealthy response for us when we face the same:

- He quickly becomes self-absorbed, referring to himself 20 times in verses 11-15.[13]
- He becomes a grumbling complainer, like the people he's meant to lead.
- He doubts God's ability to provide for the people or to change them.

13 That's 20 times in the original Hebrew: a point I first came across in Iain Duguid, *Numbers: God's Presence in the Wilderness* (Crossway, 2006), p. 151.

- He doesn't even pray for the people (which is somewhat more significant than lack of prayer on our own part, because Moses was the one who could intercede for Israel—see Deuteronomy 9:25-29).

Amazingly, the Lord is gracious to Moses. He provides vast amounts of food and also anoints elders to share the burden of leadership with Moses.

When I look at those bullet points, I feel deeply convicted. There have certainly been times when I was self-absorbed and could only see the ways I had been wronged. There have been times when I was far too ready to grumble and complain. My prayers, such as they were, became lists of irritations, and I doubted that the Lord could ever change the situation. Yet eventually, I tend to come to my senses and spend time with the Chief Shepherd until I am ready to trust that he will give me what I need to care well for the sheep.

I have found it helpful to list out the chief ways that sheep can be a trial to me, and then address them in my heart. It helps me escape from the nebulous sense of resentment. Here is my list. I know in my head that I should feel the privilege of being a shepherd, but...

1. The Needs of the Sheep Overwhelm Me

Sometimes I look around at church and don't know where to start. There are so many complicated issues bubbling away: failing marriages, disgruntled complaints, a shortage of leaders and so on (and on). I guess you feel the same sometimes. Maybe, like Moses, we need to share the load more, and so need to pray for some in the church family to grow into that. Maybe we need to accept our limitations and seek to do less. I was greatly helped years ago by reading William Still's classic book *The Work of The Pastor*, in which he observes:

> Some meddling ministers want to sort out everybody. God is not so optimistic. There are some who will die mixed-up personalities, and they may be true believers ... Don't try to do the impossible. Know your limitations.[14]

I found that incredibly liberating. There are some people that I cannot fix. There are some problems that I cannot resolve. There are some disputes that I cannot remedy. I've tried hard; I've prayed hard; but sometimes I have to accept my limitations. Maybe time and the Lord's grace will see them change; but maybe not. There are going to be times when we say to our Chief Shepherd, "Help. I can't see this person changing—so please give me grace to live with them as they are..

2. Some Sheep Falsely Accuse Me

It's hard to be in pastoral ministry for any length of time without being unfairly maligned. Of course, we do need to ensure that the accusations *are* unfair; often (not always, but sometimes) there is some kernel of truth in criticism. Some criticisms are easy to dismiss. Currently, I'm receiving three or four expletive-laden emails from one disgruntled former congregant every day. This has gone on for weeks, and the police have

---

14 William Still, *The Work of The Pastor* (Rutherford House, 1996 edition), p. 32.

told me to block them. Yet in this particular case, the emails are so bizarre that they don't really affect me. At other times, unfair accusations have come and spread in church. That hurts a lot more. When people you have known for a long time believe accusations against you without checking, that's very painful. On those occasions, the truth has emerged, and people have generally apologised. But it hurts.

3. The Sheep's Lack of Growth Frustrates Me

Most pastors feel this at some point, but again, it's worth asking ourselves what our expectations are. I recall, as a young staff member at a previous church, lamenting to the Senior Pastor about a lack of spiritual growth in one particular group. He simply laughed and said with a smile, "You do realise that's what we're here for, don't you? If the sheep all grew to maturity on their own and could defend themselves without any help, then there would be no need for shepherds. But until we reach heaven, sheep will be silly and won't always do what the shepherd wants. You'd best get used to that." Some sheep grow and mature into wonderful co-shepherds. Others remain, in John Stott's words, "wayward and obstinate".

4. Some of the Sheep have Abandoned Me

Maybe we feel this one most of all: people leaving the church, particularly those we have walked with in ministry for some time. A few families or individuals depart and we think, "How can I go on?" One of the most poignant lines throughout all of Paul's letters is 2 Timothy 1:15: "You know that everyone in the province of Asia has deserted me, including Phygelus and Hermogenes." We don't know if this was abandoning the faith or "merely" abandoning Paul and the hardships associated with his ministry. But it clearly wounded him, and it wounds under-shepherds still. Last month I pleaded with a man to repent of his affair and return to his family. He had professed faith 20 years ago after we had read the Bible together for a while. We then continued to do that for another year. Later, he joined the staff team at church for five years. I am godfather to his eldest son. My son was the ringbearer at his wedding. But now he has moved out of the family home and says he is not a Christian. It's heartbreaking. You will have your own stories.

Yet while it would not have removed the pain of people deserting the faith, the Lord had given Paul a gift: "May the Lord show mercy to the household of Onesiphorus, because he often refreshed me and was not ashamed of my chains" (v 16). It is the same for us. When discouragements of people letting us down or walking away from their faith come, it really does help to remind yourself of those in your church who are going well, serving wholeheartedly and growing in the faith—and to give thanks.

The Great Shepherd Understands Our Toil

There is nothing that we endure as shepherds that Jesus has not known to a greater depth.

Have you felt overwhelmed by the needs of the sheep? So did he:

> Then he said to them, "My soul is overwhelmed with sorrow to the point of death. Stay here and keep watch with me." (Matthew 26:38)

Have you been falsely accused? So was he:

> The chief priests and the whole Sanhedrin were looking for false evidence against Jesus so that they could put him to death. But they did not find any, though many false witnesses came forward.
> (Matthew 26:59-60)

Have you been frustrated by a lack of growth in the flock? So was he:

> Jerusalem, Jerusalem, you who kill the prophets and stone those sent to you, how often I have longed to gather your children together, as a hen gathers her chicks under her wings, and you were not willing.
> (Luke 13:34)

> He said to them, "How foolish you are, and how slow to believe all that the prophets have spoken."
> (Luke 24:25)

Have you been abandoned by those close to you in ministry? So was he:

> After a little while, those standing there went up to Peter and said, "Surely you are one of them; your accent gives you away." Then he began to call down curses, and he swore to them, "I don't know the man!" Immediately a cock crowed. (Matthew 26:73)

The Chief Shepherd knows the frustrations of caring for

sheep. "We do not have a high priest who is unable to feel sympathy for our weaknesses" (Hebrews 4:15). He knows and he understands your frustrations. Go to his throne of grace, cry out to him, and know that there you will find a sympathetic Saviour.

It helps us to remember that we can be dumb sheep too, and the Lord is still patient with us. Yes, we are shepherds, but we are sheep-like shepherds. Shepherds are also sheep—we too are those who are weak, destitute, defenceless, prone to wander, naturally unable to return and surrounded by wolves. Jesus is our Shepherd, who guides, protects, feeds, heals and restores us too. He has not finished his work in us.

Many years ago, when I was at theological college, Professor Richard Gaffin came for a week of guest lectures, and one day he was interviewed in front of the whole college by a member of the faculty. The question was put to him: "Dick, you've been training men for pastoral ministry for decades. Sat in front of you is a bunch of arrogant young guys who think their ministries are going to transform the world. What do you want to say to them?"

That, I believe, is known as a leading question. The whole room tensed up and braced for receiving a firm rebuke.

Professor Gaffin paused and then said:

> I think I want to say to you all that God isn't finished with you yet. There is more grace to come, there is more progress and sanctification to come. We all happily have a lifetime of growing closer in likeness to Jesus.

The room collectively breathed a sigh of relief. We did know that we were cocky and potentially unwise. It was a lovely encouragement. But you don't need to be self-confident, as I was (and the majority of my peer group were) to benefit from this wisdom; Dick Gaffin's encouragement is, of course, also true for those who are well aware of their own failings and full of self-doubt. God is not finished with you yet. There is more progress to come.

For myself, I know that after 25 years of ministry, I can still be stupid, cause others pain, lose my way and grow resentful. I often need to ask for forgiveness from others. So I am thoroughly grateful that my Shepherd has compassion—that he knows I'm not the finished article. And that certainly helps me to have compassion on the sheep under my care and to acknowledge that God is not finished with them.

A Glorious Task

Shepherding sheep is not easy work. It has never been easy work. It will never be easy work because sheep can be difficult. But it is wonderfully rewarding work. Let's finish this chapter with two passages that remind us of our task.

First, in Ezekiel 34, the Lord describes how he will do what the failed shepherds of Israel should have been doing:

> As a shepherd looks after his scattered flock when he is with them, so will I look after my sheep. I will rescue them from all the places where they were

> scattered on a day of clouds and darkness. I will bring them out from the nations and gather them from the countries, and I will bring them into their own land. I will pasture them on the mountains of Israel, in the ravines and in all the settlements in the land. I will tend them in a good pasture, and the mountain heights of Israel will be their grazing land. There they will lie down in good grazing land, and there they will feed in a rich pasture on the mountains of Israel. I myself will tend my sheep and have them lie down, declares the Sovereign LORD. I will search for the lost and bring back the strays. I will bind up the injured and strengthen the weak, but the sleek and the strong I will destroy. I will shepherd the flock with justice. (Ezekiel 34:12-16)

This is the work of a shepherd: to rescue the scattered; to gather them together; to tend them; to protect them; to seek for the lost and bring back the strays; to bind up the injured and to strengthen the weak.

This is the work that we are involved in all the time. I'm taking for granted that you are feeding the flock with solid food from the word of God, which has sustained people in dry seasons. Often we are unaware that believers, carrying wounds we did not know about, have, over weeks and months, been bound up and strengthened. We may not know how important it was to warn the church family against some cult that was recruiting members. But this is the task we're given, and the Lord knows and sees the shepherding we do.

Second, I sometimes turn to Luke 15:1-7 and the joy in heaven over a lost sheep returning to remind myself of the delight of my shepherding role. When someone becomes a Christian at church, I picture myself enjoying a party with Jesus in heaven and hear him saying, *See, isn't this job that I've given to you the best in the world?* But I also stretch the picture further to include anyone at church who is striving to "live a life worthy of the Lord and please him in every way" (Colossians 1:10). I picture the rejoicing in heaven over a long-term believer stepping up and serving in a new way; or over a young widow trusting in the Lord through the unexpected loss of her husband; or over a young man giving up his secular career to become a shepherd. Again, I hear Jesus say, *What could be better than this? I am using you as my under-shepherd to bring joy to heaven.*

You and I have been entrusted with caring for the Lord's most treasured possession. When we help the sheep return to the fold, and when we see them healed, protected and strengthened, we are the means of bringing joy to heaven.

Do let yourself smile at that.

Chapter 3

There Is No Greater Task

"There is no greater task a man can perform in the whole world than this, that he is being used to release the all-searching word of God upon a company of needy souls. It is the most amazing thing. It works! God works. His word works. Prayer works. The Spirit works."[15]

"There is no greater task ... in the whole world." Let me repeat that: *There is no greater task.*

I think that most of us know the truth of this idea: that preaching the Bible is a privilege. For me and for many of my peers, it was the joy and privilege of teaching the Scriptures, and above all preaching, that drew us into ministry. Having preached more than a thousand sermons, I would admit that while there are moments when I know this, there are also plenty of times when I need to be reminded that it is true.

In the last chapter, we began to see that central to

---

15 William Still, *The Work of the Pastor*, p. 22.

the work of shepherding was teaching the sheep the Scriptures. John Owen put it starkly:

> The principal work of ministers is to "preach the Word ... in season and out of season" [2 Timothy 4:2] to increase the knowledge of God, and of our Lord and Saviour Jesus Christ, in the church, by all means. "I will give you shepherds ... who will feed you with knowledge and understanding" (Jeremiah 3:15). Any who take it upon themselves to be pastors, and who neglect this work of feeding the flock, might as well, with less work, and equal modesty, renounce Jesus Christ.[16]

This is serious. And this is what Jesus modelled to us. We're told in Mark 6:34 that...

> ... when Jesus landed and saw a large crowd, he had compassion on them, because they were like sheep without a shepherd. So he began teaching them many things.

Of course he did. Sheep without a shepherd are leaderless, aimless and vulnerable (Numbers 27:15-17; 1 Kings 22:17), and so the Chief Shepherd taught them. Given what Jesus has said and done so far in Mark's Gospel, that must mean that he taught them who he was and that he stressed and showed them their need of him to forgive their sins and to bring resurrection life.

We have the enormous privilege of feeding God's sheep with his word. It is, of course, non-negotiable that it is with his word. I pity ministers who lack biblical

---

16 John Owen, *Gospel Ministry* (Banner of Truth, 2023), p. 45.

convictions and so attempt to feed a congregation with their own thoughts. I would hate the idea of shuffling around in the dust of my own opinions and presenting them as a sermon (as, I hope, would my congregation). But wonderfully, God has spoken, and our task is to speak his words, communicating to others what he has communicated to us.

It is extraordinary that God uses us for this. *There is no greater task.*

Paid to Sit at Jesus' Feet

Before we get to the task of proclamation, it is worth pausing on the amazing fact that we are given a salary[17] to sit at Jesus' feet and learn from him. The time that we get to spend in the Bible is amazing!

After a few years, it's easy to take this for granted. I often try to force myself to remember the years when I was in secular employment and my devotional times were at 6 a.m., when I was bleary-eyed and half-asleep. I would long for holidays, which tended to be the only time I could get into a meaty Christian book. Now, what was once squeezed around the edges of work *is* my work. For instance, I'm currently trying to spend a few hours a week doing some background work on the Song of Songs, ahead of preaching it in a few months' time. I am, at points, a little bewildered in my study (it's quite tricky!), but what a blessing. Lots of people at church have given money so that I get to grapple with God's word and dig away in it to discover treasures

---

17 Or a stipend, or funding to be employed in ministry.

that I had never previously seen. Amazing! In a highly vivid picture, William Perkins suggests that our job is to spend so much time in the word that we "eat it":

> A minister must be a divine interpreter, an interpreter of God's meaning. And therefore, he must not only read the book but eat it. He must not only have the knowledge of divine things flowing in his brain but engraved on his heart and printed in his soul by the spiritual finger of God. To this end, after all his own study, meditation and discussion, his use of commentaries and other human helps, he must pray with David, "Open my eyes, that I may see wondrous things from your law."[18]

There's a challenge there—yet also, how staggering that many in our churches *want us* to do *this*! They want us to study and meditate on Scripture, to spend time praying for insight, and to read helpful books, so that the knowledge of divine things flows in our brains and is engraved in our heart. Lots of people at your church are driving trucks and battling spreadsheets and enduring unreasonable bosses and trying to sell products partly so that you can spend time studying God's word. Surely this is one of the chief perks of our role.

The Mouthpiece of God

Paul wrote, "We are ambassadors for Christ, God making his appeal through us" (2 Corinthians 5:20, ESV). When

---

18 William Perkins, *The Art of Prophesying and the Calling of the Ministry* (Banner of Truth, revised edition 2021), p. 101. Presumably he is influenced here by Ezekiel 3:1-3.

we stand up and preach, God uses the feeble jars of clay that we are from which to shine forth the gospel of Christ to his people. We stand between heaven and earth, between the divine and the human, and proclaim, "Thus says the Lord". That is a truth that should make us fear and tremble. It is a truth that should send us fleeing to the Lord in prayer to ask for his mercy on us and his assistance for us. Yet it is a truth that should also make us delight in wonder: "Who am I, Lord, that you would use me to declare your glory, to feed your sheep, to bring the dead to life?"

Years ago, after leaving secular work but before going to theological college, I was a ministry intern alongside a few other guys in a local church. One of the guys, whom I'll call Wayne, was godly and super-competent, and the best preacher among the interns. His only problem was that every time he was due to preach, he would spend half an hour before the service vomiting. The sermons were great, but the thought of what he was doing—the responsibility of it and the weightiness of the task—were too much. He became a magnificent lay elder. But when I look back, while I don't want that debilitating experience, I do think Wayne understood something that I didn't: being God's mouthpiece is a solemn charge and an awesome privilege.

To proclaim God's word is not an occupation or Sunday hobby. It is not an opportunity for self-expression or self-fulfilment. It is not *merely* an explanation of truth or an unveiling of facts. It is the trumpeting of eternity-changing news; it is the heralding of the greatness of Christ; it is the proclamation of God's word for transformation.[19]

The overlap between the word of God and the work of the preacher is extraordinary. To take one example of two similar verses in 2 Timothy, Paul writes:

> All Scripture is breathed out by God and profitable for teaching, for reproof, for correction, and for training in righteousness. (3:16, ESV)
>
> Preach the word; be ready in season and out of season; reprove, rebuke, and exhort, with complete patience and teaching. (4:2, ESV)

Let's line those up:

teaching,	reproof,	correction,	training in righteousness
reprove,	rebuke,	exhort,	with complete patience and teaching.

The similarity is striking. William Perkins puts it this way:

---

19 I would subscribe to the view that there is a difference between preaching and teaching. Of the three primary New Testament verbs for preaching (*kerysso* = preach/herald 59x; *euangelizomai* = preach good news 54x; *katangello* = proclaim/announce 18x), all have the sense of a public proclamation of momentous news or great importance. While preaching will always include teaching, the difference is in the urgent call to respond. Preaching is always designed to elicit a response, not merely inform. However, there is overlap between public proclamation and individual or small-group teaching. In his preaching (*katangello*), Paul admonishes, and so should believers (Colossians 1:28; 1 Thessalonians 5:12-14; Colossians 3:16; Hebrews 3:13). There is a sense in which this ministry flows out of the public proclamation of the word.

> Notice the sympathy and cooperation there is between the heart of God and the task of the minister. Man preaches and God blesses; man works on the heart and God gives grace; the minister expounds righteousness and God says, "So be it, he shall be righteous"; a minister pronounces mercy to a penitent sinner and immediately God has mercy on him ... It is a considerable honour for ministers and for their ministry that God himself blesses it and works when they work.[20]

We proclaim God's words. We stand as his heralds. In vivid language, Edward Reynolds observes how the Lord preaches and encourages us to do the same:

> In that great work of men's conversion unto God, he is said to allure them and to speak comfortably to them, to beseech them and to persuade them, to set forth Christ to the soul as altogether lovely, as the fairest of ten thousand, as the desire of the nations, as the riches of the world, that men might be inflamed to love the beauty of holiness (Hosea 2:14; 2 Corinthians 5:17; Song of Songs 5:10, 16; Haggai 2:7; Romans 11:12; Ephesians 5:8; 1 Timothy 1:15).[21]

We are those privileged to do this as God's mouthpiece. *There is no greater task.*

---

20 William Perkins, *The Art of Prophesying and the Calling of the Ministry*, p. 123-124.

21 Edward Reynolds, *A Treatise on the Passions and Faculties of the Soul* (London: Robert Boulter, 1678), p. 619.

Performing Miracles

The Lord uses our preaching to open the eyes of the blind and bring the dead to life (2 Corinthians 4:4-6; Ephesians 2:1-10). That's extraordinary. He uses us to bring transformation to those who are already believers. Of course, I've not forgotten Newton's hymn from chapter 1:

> Who can describe the pain
> Which faithful preachers feel,
> Constrain'd to preach in vain
> To hearts as hard as steel?
> Or who can tell the pleasures felt
> When stubborn hearts begin to melt?

I'm sure we've all had the experience of feeling that we're preaching in vain. I'm sometimes reminded of a colleague back when I was a schoolteacher, who wrote on a pupil's report card, "Trying to teach Jeremy is like trying to plant seeds of grain on a well-polished cliff of granite". (He was told to amend this somewhat damning comment.) There are some occasions when I think I'm trying to plant the seed of God's word on some pretty hardened cliffs. Yet we do also see stubborn hearts melt. It is a glorious moment for a pastor when someone comes up to us after a sermon and says, "You were preaching that to me, weren't you?" The answer is no, we weren't; but yes, God's Spirit was, through us. God's word is at work and addresses the heart to bring transformation.

If you're at a stage of feeling a little jaded by the lack of visible fruit from your preaching, you need a reminder that the Bible is...

- a hammer that breaks the rock into pieces (Jeremiah 23:29)—it is able to shatter pride, resistance to sin and stubbornness in a person's heart, even after decades.
- a fire that burns, consumes and purifies (Jeremiah 23:29)—it can cleanse the worst of sinners.
- like a small seed that appears to be tiny but contains life and can grow exponentially (Matthew 13).
- living and active (Hebrews 4:12). As Martin Luther commented, "The Bible is alive, it speaks to me; it has feet, it runs after me; it has hands, it lays hold of me".

I don't get vast numbers of thankful cards or emails, but I treasure this one, which a former church member sent to me after I had spoken at a weekend away for her church. I have her permission to quote it:

> Hi Matt,
> Seeing you last week was a real challenge to me also to reflect on the time I had spent in London, hearing you preach God's word each week at a time of my life that needed it so much. I had been battling sexual sin and a relationship with a non-Christian at the time and it took me a long time to reach out for accountability or help—I just lived in my denial, guilt and shame. Many things you said in your sermons on Sunday rang in my ears during the week. Slowly through the truth of the gospel, I see

> how God has changed my heart to hear those words of rebuke as joyful music, hope and God's love for his children, away from guilt and shame and into his forgiveness and a new life. The thought of a non-Christian relationship is now so unappealing, even horrid to me, in a way I never would have thought I could feel.
>
> I am so amazed by God's love and grace and provision. He truly never lets us go, no matter how far we ourselves try to run (and oh, how we run!).

I had no idea of any of this at the time when she was listening to my sermons week by week. God's word silently did its miraculous work of changing a life through the stumbling words of an ignorant preacher. I trust that similar miracles are happening all the time that I am utterly unaware of. I'm sure they're happening in your church too. There are days when we wonder if we're doing anything of any use at all, but often God is at work unseen through the word that we have planted in people's heads and hearts on Sunday.

Of course, there are also times when we do get to see the Lord perform miracles when we speak as his heralds. Some are born again in front of us. Believers have their lives transformed:

> There is no greater task a man can perform in the whole world than this, that he is being used to release the all-searching word of God upon a company of needy souls.[22]

---

22 William Still, *The Work of the Pastor*, p. 22.

Equipping God's People

Paul tells us that "Christ himself gave the apostles, the prophets, the evangelists, the pastors and teachers, to equip his people for works of service, so that the body of Christ may be built up" (Ephesians 4:11-12). That, again, is a striking truth. You are a gift to your church! The role of pastor-teachers is to equip or prepare people. The Greek word translated "equip", *katartizō*, has two broad senses to it: to repair and to train. Consider these other uses—the same root form is italicised:

> Going on from there, he saw two other brothers, James son of Zebedee and his brother John. They were in a boat with their father Zebedee, *mending* their nets. Jesus called them. (Matthew 4:21)

> The student is not above the teacher, but everyone who is fully *trained* will be like their teacher.
> (Luke 6:40)

> Brothers and sisters, if someone is caught in a sin, you who live by the Spirit should *restore* that person gently. But watch yourselves, or you also may be tempted. (Galatians 6:1)

> Night and day we pray most earnestly that we may see you again and *supply* what is lacking in your faith.
> (1 Thessalonians 3:10)

That is what happens when we teach the Bible. God takes what we say from his word and equips in two senses. First, he restores us sinners who have been bent out of shape both by our own sin and how we have been sinned against. He mends the broken thoughts, ambitions and desires we have developed over time. In this sense, a preacher is like a doctor. Secondly, the Lord prepares us to effectively serve him; he trains us in godliness and supplies what is lacking in knowledge, affection and direction. So, in this sense, a preacher is like a teacher or mentor.

Yet what must give us pause, once again, is that God uses us for this task. We are the gift he gives to the church to equip the body to grow to maturity. How extraordinary.

Being the mouthpiece of God, the means of miraculous change, the gift that equips the church—this *is* wonderful, but it is also somewhat terrifying. Writing this chapter has reminded me vividly of Wayne's apprehension and physical response. There must be a sense in which that is right. Richard Baxter would remind us:

> This is not a burden for the shoulders of a child. What skill does every part of our work require! ... To preach a sermon, I think, is not the hardest part, and yet what skill is necessary to make the truth plain, to convince the hearers, to let irresistible light into their consciences, and to keep it there and drive all home; to screw the truth into their minds and work Christ into their affections, to meet every objection, and clearly resolve it, to drive sinners to a stand and make them see that there is no hope, but that they must unavoidably either be converted or condemned ... This, and a great deal more that

> should be done in every sermon, must surely require a great deal of holy skill.[23]

He's right! This is a challenging task. Yet it is one entrusted to us, and we can trust that the Lord will equip us for that task. "My word that goes out from my mouth," God says, and it goes out through his heralds, his prophets and preachers: "It will not return to me empty, but will accomplish what I desire and achieve the purpose for which I sent it" (Isaiah 55:11).

The Best Preacher Your Church Can Have

You are Christ's gift to your church. And this is a gift to your *specific* church. God has given you to the local church where you are based. You and I may not be "great preachers"; few are. But you are the best preacher that your congregation can have, because you are *their* preacher. I've often been struck that in Acts 20 Paul uses the same verb twice of his preaching. He did not "hesitate" or "shrink back":

> You know that I have *not hesitated* to preach anything that would be helpful to you but have taught you publicly and from house to house. (v 20)
>
> I have *not hesitated* to proclaim to you the whole will of God. (v 27)

Paul wanted to give them the "full counsel of God" (v 27, ESV): a balanced diet of biblical genres and a refusal to miss out truths unpalatable to his audience.

---

23 Richard Baxter, *The Reformed Pastor*, p. 70.

Every pastor should have this resolve and could presumably carry it out in any church.

Yet Paul also took time to preach what was useful to the church in Ephesus. There must have been something people-specific to this preaching, especially as he followed it up by visiting from house to house. Paul thought about what was specifically useful for the context in Ephesians (probably often related to the city's obsession with power and magic). This required some knowledge of those people and that place; the itinerant preacher could not have performed this role. A good preacher has to be involved in the lives of people, and this is why, in many ways, *you* are the best preacher that *your* people can have, because you know them and know what is useful for them.

To caricature somewhat, you could be at a pastors' conference and listen to a sermon that you personally find staggeringly good. You might think, "I'm going to repeat that in my church". But it will probably misfire, because most of your church are not full-time pastors. Knowing the audience matters! Most of us are unknown preachers in unknown places, but we do know the people gathered at our church on Sunday, and they know us. We are involved in their lives, they see that we love them, and this builds up a trust in our preaching over time. I take it that this is why, when Paul tells the Ephesians elders that he will never see them again, they cry. He has not merely taught the Scriptures; he has taught the Scriptures to *them*.

John Owen observed the splendour of being a pastor in a local context:

> There is greater glory in giving a minister to a poor congregation than there is in the instalment and enthroning of all the popes, cardinals and metropolitans of the world, whatever their glory might be. Christ is seen in his theatre of glory in the communication of this office and these officers.[24]

Isn't that great?! Under God's hand, our church in London has grown over the past few decades, but I still remember well preaching to a room with 20 or 30 people in it. At that time, and still sometimes today, I needed to remember to live by faith, not by sight—to be reminded that it was a glorious role to be given, more glorious than a coronation.

There are multiple occasions when I have turned back to this fantastic letter that John Newton sent to his friend and mentor Alexander Clunie, requesting prayer from him:

> How fast the weeks return—we are again upon the eve of a Sabbath. May the Lord give us much of his own Spirit on his own day. I trust I have a remembrance in your prayers. I need them much—my service is great. It is, indeed, no small thing to stand between God and the people—to divide the word of truth aright—to give every one portion—to withstand the counter tides of opposition and popularity—and to press those truths upon others, the power of which, I, at times, feel so little of in my own soul. A cold, corrupt heart is uncomfortable company in the pulpit. Yet in the midst of all my

24 John Owen, *Gospel Ministry,* p. 48.

> fears and unworthiness, I am enabled to cleave to the promise, and to rely on the power of the great Redeemer. I know I am engaged in the cause against which the gates of hell cannot prevail. If he died and rose again, if he ever lives to make intercession—there must be safety under the shadow of his wings: there would I lie. In his name I would lift up my banner; in his strength I would go forth, do what he enables me, then take shame to myself that I can do no better, and put my hand upon my mouth, confessing that I am dust and ashes, less than the least of all his mercies.[25]

If you've read that quote quickly, please read it again. I think Newton describes me so well: my weakness and my fear and also, at times, the coldness of my heart. Yet also he reminds us of the glory of the task and God's power to work through jars of clay.

So, keep going. "There is no greater task a man can perform in the whole world than this, that he is being used to release the all-searching word of God upon a company of needy souls."

25 John Newton. "Letter XL," 26 July 1766 in *The Christian Correspondent or a series of Religious Letters, written by The Rev. John Newton to Captain Alex. Clunie, from the year 1761, to the death of the latter in 1770* (Hull: Printed by George Prince, 1790).

Chapter 4

Contemplating Christ

In *The Glory of Christ*, John Owen asks a poignant question:

> Do any of us find decays in grace prevailing in us: deadness, coldness, lukewarmness, a kind of spiritual stupidity and senselessness coming upon us?

Yes, I do. There are seasons when I feel jaded and weary and find myself serving without a great deal of joy. Yes, I do have times when "decays in grace" prevail. When that is the case, Owen continues:

> Let us assure ourselves there is no better way for our healing and deliverance, yea, no other way but this alone, namely, the obtaining of a fresh view of the glory of Christ by faith, and a steady abiding therein. Constant contemplation of Christ and his glory, putting forth its transforming power unto the revival of all grace, is the only relief in this case.[26]

---

26 John Owen, *"The Glory of Christ"*, Vol. 1 of *The Works of John Owen*, ed. William H. Goold (Banner of Truth, 1965 reprint), p. 395.

I imagine that most of us have discovered this truth (although we may not have expressed it this eloquently): we need a constant contemplation of Christ and his glory.

I do know this in my head. I'm confident that you know it too. Yet, somehow, I can fail to actually make time for that contemplation of Christ, or (more commonly) I can sit in a chair and read my Bible and yet have my mind elsewhere.

Maybe that's not you at all. Perhaps you're in no sense lukewarm, but you do spend a significant amount of time bewildered. I'm regularly struck by how many pastors, when you begin to actually chat honestly, will say something like "I have no idea what I'm doing really". Twice in the past month, pastors who are both older than me and have been in ministry longer than me have said, "I do wonder if I should resign. I don't seem to be achieving anything." From the outside, these are godly and well-respected men whom people would assume are confident due to long and fruitful ministries. Yet inside, they're discouraged. Owen's advice in this situation was...

> A due contemplation of the glory of Christ will restore and compose the mind ... [It] will lift the minds and hearts of believers above all the troubles of this life, and is the sovereign antidote that will expel all the poison that is in them; which otherwise might perplex and enslave their souls.[27]

Owen wrote these words having buried ten children and lived through the incredibly complicated times of

27 As above, p. 279.

the mid-17th-century English Civil Wars. He had many reasons for a distressed mind. Yet his simple remedy in tricky times was "contemplate Christ".

This is the great need of all believers—but for pastors, the temptation to discouragement in ministry is more acute and always present. So we need to take heed of Owen's antidote all the more. And the great thing is that we have all the more opportunity to enact his advice because those of us in paid ministry have churches full of believers who want us to spend our time contemplating Christ. What a gift! As we touched upon in the last chapter, we are paid to sit at the feet of Jesus and learn from him. Richard Baxter put it like this:

> What an excellent privilege it is, to live in studying ... Christ! To be continually searching into his mysteries or feeding on them! To be daily employed in the consideration of the blessed nature, works and ways of God! Others are glad of the leisure of the Lord's Day and now and then, of an hour besides, when they can lay hold upon it. But we may keep a continual Sabbath. We may do almost nothing else, but study and talk of God and glory, engage in acts of prayer and praise, and drink in his sacred, saving truths. Our employment is all high and spiritual. Whether we be alone or in company, our business is for another world. Oh, that our hearts were but more tuned to this work![28]

28 Richard Baxter, *The Reformed Pastor* (Banner of Truth, 1999), p. 128.

So, in this chapter, I really am simply going to say to readers who are in professional Christian ministry, "Make sure that you enjoy time contemplating Christ in the Scriptures and responding to him in prayer". That may seem startlingly obvious and therefore unnecessary—except that, if you are anything like me, you find yourself looking at God's word and praying dutifully but not delightedly. Or you read and understand a text, but you don't read and then meditate and enjoy Christ.

Sometimes we meet with Jesus dutifully and find that delight emerges. But sometimes—often—we do have to work at turning duty into delight. I've always been struck by this observation of Thomas Watson:

> Study is a duty, but meditation is a higher duty; study is the finding out of a truth, meditation is the spiritual improvement of a truth; the one searcheth for the vein of gold, the other digs out the gold. Study is like a winter sun that hath little warmth and influence; meditation melts the heart when it is frozen, and makes it drop into tears of love. Meditation is the bellows of the affections. Meditation without study is dangerous; divinity is not to be obtained by inspiration. Study without meditation is barren and fruitless. The end of study is to make us more accurate in our thoughts; the end of meditation is to make us more holy in our affections. Study and meditation, like two turtles, must be coupled together; the one makes the other fruitful.[29]

---

29 Thomas Watson, *Taking Heaven by Storm* (Banner of Truth, 2000 edition), p. 25.

Hear him rightly—"meditation without study is dangerous". He is not suggesting speculative theological daydreamings. Yet at the same time, "study without meditation is barren and fruitless"—and that is sometimes what my own devotions can become.

The Pleasure of Devotional Time

When have you had the best season of "quiet times" or "devotions"? I assume that, for most of us, they ebb and flow somewhat. Some days we can barely remember what we've read in the fog of tiredness or to the background of screaming children or when inhibited by a distracted mind, flitting from task to task. But there are other days when you soar on wings like eagles: you know you've really met with the Lord, have heard him speak from his word, and have found your prayers of response are fulsome and emotive and heartfelt.

I think my answer to the question of when my quiet times are at their best is "When I have unrushed time". There are seasons when I can make unrushed time; I get up earlier while the house is quiet. There are also seasons when it is very hard to carve out such time, and I make do with mediocre time with the Lord. But I know I can't let that rumble on for too long. I need to contemplate Christ. I need to behold my God.

One season when I learned this again was in the madness of the Covid pandemic. After the initial novelty of working from home with family around wore off, I found it a wretched time. It coincided with the death of my parents and, overall, I slowly went a little bit crazy. Yet one upside was that there was more time available, and possibly the most useful thing I did in that strange couple of years was invest time in the book of Isaiah. The vivid imagery of the book lends itself well to meditation and digging out gold. Indeed we are ordered to contemplate him—98 times we are commanded to "behold your God" / "behold him." This is particularly in focus in the much-loved chapter 40. We're told there exactly what the people were saying—the Lord asks:

> Why do you complain, Jacob? Why do you say, Israel, "My way is hidden from the LORD; my cause is disregarded by my God"? (Isaiah 40:27)

They are effectively asking, *Don't you care, Lord? Don't you see our distress?* Jerusalem had been destroyed by the Babylonians and the people taken off into exile as captives. So it is understandable why the people would ask, *Don't you care?* In response, the Lord tells a broken and disillusioned people, suffering after invasion, deportation and humiliation, that they need to "behold him" (four times in this chapter). Here, then, is the answer for when we're tired or weary:

> Do you not know? Have you not heard? The LORD is the everlasting God, the Creator of the ends of the earth. He will not grow *tired* or *weary*, and his understanding no one can fathom. He gives strength to the *tired*[30] and increases the power of the weak.
>
> Even youths grow *tired* and *weary*, and young men stumble and fall; but those who hope in the LORD

30 I've changed the NIV translation here to reflect the same Hebrew root which is used three times, as is the Hebrew "weary".

> will renew their strength. They will soar on wings like eagles; they will run and not grow *weary*, they will walk and not be faint. (v 29-31)

We need to contemplate—to behold—our God. We need to recognise his glories. He is so unlike us. We're locked in time, but he is eternal. We're local in thinking, but he has global vision. We grow tired, but he has boundless energy. We get confused, but he has fathomless wisdom. We need refreshing, but he is endless refreshment. Brothers and sisters, we really do need to meditate on who he is until we are strengthened to keep going. And, wonderfully, we are *paid* to meditate upon him.

A healthy church family knows that having a pastor in good health—physically, emotionally and spiritually—is good for them. A healthy church wants the pastor's work to be a joy and not a burden, for that is of no benefit to them (Hebrews 13:17). Thoughtful Christians know that their pastor needs, in Owen's language, "a due contemplation of the glory of Christ to restore and compose the mind".

Time with Jesus is good for you, and it is good for your church.

Letting Others Help Us Contemplate

There may be times when we need the assistance of others in our devotions. I'm sure lots of us will use commentaries. Yet don't forget Watson's caution. Study will be but a winter sun with little warmth unless we have meditated until our hearts are melted. In my background study for the Song of Songs, I enjoyed

Sinclair Ferguson's observations on John Owen's short commentary. I'll quote it at some length:

> What did Owen think he was doing in his exposition of the Song of Solomon? He did not think he was creating his doctrine of Christ from its pages. But he did think it was an illustration of the fellowship which the believer enjoys with his Lord ... it is, in other words, a transcript of the affections of the child of God ... [Here] is this man, with his massive intellectual equipment, his great grasp of theology—and what is he looking for most of all? It is the sense of the love of Christ for him. That is what he sees he needs if he is to progress in Christian piety. Surely there is something for us to learn here. We eschew the false dichotomy between the Person of Christ and the Bible which reveals him. We know of no other Christ than the one we meet in the pages of Scripture. But it is all too possible to search the Scriptures which testify of Christ, and never actually to discover the power of their truth in coming to Christ, and drinking in his love for us.[31]

I'm conscious of being on slightly risky ground here. All of us will have different temperaments, and I don't want to project myself onto you. Personally (at the risk of indulging in stereotypes) I'm not a passionate Welshman or an enthusiastic Kenyan. I'm an Englishman—I may be a little more "heart-on-sleeve" than your average English evangelical, but you won't

31 Sinclair Ferguson, "John Owen on Christian Piety" in *Some Pastors and Teachers* (Banner of Truth, 2017), p. 286.

catch me dancing in church. Yet I know that one thing I need when I meet with Jesus is to be "drinking in his love for us", because "us" includes "me".

When I became a Christian at university, my favourite verse was Philippians 3:8:

> I consider everything a loss compared to the surpassing greatness of knowing Christ Jesus my Lord. (NIV 1984)

It was my password for everything—bank accounts, credit cards… (Revealing this will not help any criminals—it was 35 years ago.) I really *felt* that truth deeply. These days, there are still times when I still feel that this is undoubtedly true, and there are also times when I don't live or think that way. Perhaps the righteousness that Christ has won for me has become over-familiar. But, a little while ago, I read Samuel Rutherford's meditation on Philippians 3:8, and it helped me enormously:

> Then after this day, convene all your lovers before your soul, and give them their leave; and strike hands with Christ, that thereafter there may be no happiness to you but Christ, no hunting for anything but Christ, no bed at night, when death cometh, but Christ. Christ, Christ, who but Christ! …
>
> I gave nothing for Christ. And now I protest before men and angels that Christ cannot be exchanged, that Christ cannot be sold, that Christ cannot be weighed. Where would angels, or all the world, find a balance to weigh him in? All lovers blush when ye

> stand beside Christ! Woe upon all love but the love of Christ! Hunger, hunger for evermore be upon all heaven but Christ! Shame, shame for evermore be upon all glory but Christ's glory. I cry death, death upon all lives but the life of Christ.[32]

His style of writing may not be to everyone's taste, but there's something about grappling with his words that makes me engage with the Bible text more deeply and contemplate Christ more profoundly. Sometimes we can all benefit from the writings of others to help us take advantage of the fact that, as pastors, we have time set aside to contemplate and delight in the Lord.

Don't Let Satan Win

I may be a little eccentric (or just influenced by C.S. Lewis), but there are plenty of times when I ask, "What would Satan want?" and then seek to do the opposite. So, when I'm feeling discouraged, I remind myself that Satan is delighted by that—and that's the kick I need to cheer up. Or maybe I'm finding service a burden and am a little resentful. I tell myself that Satan has achieved his task. And so I remind myself that I don't want to let him win! At the beginning of *The Screwtape Letters*, Lewis cautions us, "Readers are advised to remember the devil is a liar."[33]

---

32 Samuel Rutherford, "Letter LXXX (to Marion M'Naught, on his comfort under tribulation, prison as a palace)—Aberdeen, 1637" in *Letters of Samuel Rutherford,* (Banner of Truth, 2006). I feel the need to warn you that Rutherford is probably not the place to start if you're unfamiliar with Puritan writings. He is far more comfortable speaking of the kisses and love-blinks of Christ than many of us in the 21st century might be.

33 C.S. Lewis, *The Screwtape Letters* (Harper Collins, 2009), Preface, p. x.

Some of the lies that arrive in my head frequently and that I'm tempted to listen to are...

> You're a fraud. You are not qualified or equipped to be a pastor.
>
> You're wasting your time. You should go and find something else to do.
>
> Nothing of worth has been achieved.
>
> Unless you are a phenomenal minister, there is no point in doing ministry. (Steady plodders are of no use in the kingdom.)

The danger of these lies is that they are so easily believed and there is partial truth in them. What I need to do is remind myself of the rest of the truth:

> I'll never be as well equipped as a pastor as I would want. BUT I have the Lord, I have the Scriptures and I can pray. I did spend a number of years receiving formal training, and others think I'm qualified.
>
> There are times when I do seem to have invested time on projects and in people with no discernible fruit. BUT I have done it for the Lord and so, as with the woman who poured perfume on Jesus' feet, I have done what I can, and Jesus will remember this (Mark 14:9).
>
> There are seasons when I cannot see what has been achieved. BUT taking the long view, people have become Christians, others have kept going in the faith and still others have borne fruit.

> Okay, steady plodders don't achieve as much as "the great ones". BUT I read Romans 16 and find a long list of names commended and have no idea what they actually did. However, Paul thinks that they are worthy of praise.

If we fail to spend time contemplating Christ, then these lies become far more believable to us. We need time with him.

And sometimes we need help from others. Back in April 2021, I hit the wall. The combination of managing the church and staff through Covid and navigating the death of my parents had left me exhausted, and I was ordered by our elders to take some time off. I remember taking a long walk around a local park with one of them and lamenting that I was exhausted and done. I couldn't see myself returning to ministry full time and so was daydreaming about what else I should do. He listened a while and then said:

> So, you're physically and emotionally exhausted. Does that seem like the best time to take a life-changing decision? Matt, what would you say to someone in your situation? Would you encourage them to make a dramatic change? Or would you say, "Go away, rest, and spend time with the Lord?" Now, go away and spend some extended time with the Lord. Pray that he restores you. And let's meet up regularly so that I can check you're not taking rash decisions while you're off-kilter.

He was speaking sense. I *was* deeply exhausted, and I did need some rest. Yet also, I needed to resist the temptation to give in to self-pity. That would have been a win for Satan.

I have been helped by returning occasionally to this reflection of Newton's on the clause in the Lord's Prayer, "Lead us not into temptation". He writes of our need to be deliberate in praying this request:

> The subtlety and power of this adversary are very great: he is an over-match for us; and we have no hope of safety but in the Lord's protection ... We are not to expect an absolute freedom from temptation; we are to be called soldiers, and must sometimes meet with enemies, and perhaps with wounds; yet considering this prayer as provided by him, who knows what we are, and where we are, it may afford us both instruction and consolation ... I am one among many who have suffered greatly for want of paying more attention to my need of this prayer.[34]

I am another who has suffered for want of praying this prayer! Owen writes in a similar vein:

> If we do not abide in prayer, we will abide in temptation. Let this be one aspect of our daily intercession: "God, preserve my soul, and keep my heart and all its ways so that I will not be entangled." When this is true in our lives, a passing temptation will not overcome us. We will remain free while others lie in bondage.[35]

---

34 John Newton, *The Works of John Newton,* Vol. 1 (Banner of Truth, 2018), p. 383, 387.

35 John Owen, *Works,* Vol. 6: *Temptation and Sin* (Banner of Truth, 1968 edition), p. 127.

Brothers and sisters, we have this great resource: a Lord who calls us to cast our burdens upon him, our discouragements upon him, our wounds upon him. He can and he will strengthen us to resist the temptation to dwell in discouragement, resentment or self-pity.

Praying for the Church

Of course, you know that you're called not only to pray for yourself but for others. You'll know (and perhaps be prompted to feel privately a little guilty) that when the apostles were set apart in Acts 6, they promised, "We will devote ourselves to prayer and the ministry of the word" (6:4, ESV). An honest personal assessment would be that I am devoted to the ministry of the word and I pray regularly. But *devoted* to prayer or giving it the same attention as teaching the Bible? That is more variable. Sometimes, when I feel helpless, then yes—devoted. At other times, I'm really not sure that "devotion" is the right word. Fortunately (I think I mean that word), the Lord causes me to fail or to hit brick walls frequently enough that prayer rises again as a priority. Stuck on my pinboard above my desk is this reminder...

> Satan will not be charmed out of his possessions: we must lay siege to the souls of sinners, which are his garrison.[36]

I need reminding that spiritual work is supernatural. Conversion, repentance in believers, a transformed

36 John Newton, *The Works of John Newton,* Vol. 1, p. 149.

mind—these are all miraculous works, and we get to (and need to) pray for these miracles. Our churches have set us apart to pray for them.

Again, Satan would love us to be discouraged if we realise we lack devotion to prayer. I've found in ministry that my constant mistake is to aim for perfection and then be wildly discouraged when I fall short. I've come to think that it's a cunning strategy of Satan's to...

1. set up an impossible standard for me, so that...

2. I fall short of this standard, and...

3. I don't bother at all (because it's all or nothing).

Personally, I've now learned that *progress* is great (see 1 Timothy 4:15 and chapter 7 of this book). Being honest, do you rarely ever pray for your people? Then five minutes a day is a win. Do you currently pray for 5-10 minutes a day? Then 15 minutes is victory! Do you tend to pray once a day? Then twice a day is great. Wherever you're at, you can make progress.

Praying for the supernatural work of God in people's lives is essential because we're in a spiritual battle. But praying for our churches is also essential to maintain our own hearts in the ministry, as John Owen reminds us:

> I do not believe that any minister, any pastor in the world, can maintain a proper love for his church if he does not pray for them. He will meet with so many provocations, follies and injuries that nothing will be able to maintain a warm love in his heart towards

> them without continual prayer in their behalf. Such prayer conquers all prejudices.[37]

I appreciate his honesty. Truly there are a lot of "provocations, follies and injuries". Only prayer can maintain our love!

Praying Beyond the Church

If most of us feel a little guilty when we read of the apostles devoting themselves to prayer, we probably also feel our shortcomings when we read of Paul telling the Ephesian church, "I have not stopped giving thanks for you, remembering you in my prayers" (Ephesians 1:16). But again, we have the privilege of being given time to pray for individuals, fellow pastors and other churches, mission partners, the nation and world. I *love* getting updates from mission partners—I can see in their progress the fruit of my prayers. You spend a year or two praying for the mysteriously titled "G and P", who are Muslims reading the Bible with a mission partner in Oman, and then the wondrous news comes that "G" and his family are now professing faith. It's thrilling! There are times when there seems to be little progress in our own churches here, but to play a role in praying for ministry elsewhere and hearing of answered prayers *there* is massively encouraging.

I've been inspired by James Outram Fraser in this regard. If you're unfamiliar with him, he was a missionary in China in the first part of the 20th century. His work was focused on the Lisu tribe in a mountainous region.

37 John Owen, *Gospel Ministry*, p. 80.

There was a season of nearly two years when, due to political unrest, warring tribes and appalling weather, travel through the mountain passes was impossible, and Fraser was completely cut off from the Lisu believers. He couldn't even reach them by letter. His diaries record his struggles with loneliness, doubt and the temptation to give up and return to England. Yet there came a moment of revelation when he realised that nothing could stop his prayers or the prayers of those back in England who were supporting him. He summarised this newly found conviction:

> I am feeling more and more that it is after all just the prayers of God's people that call down blessing upon the work ... whether they are engaged in the field or not.[38]

When Fraser was eventually able to get through the mountains and return to the Lisu again, he discovered that many of the believers had remained faithful. Indeed, they had stepped up to lead in his absence, setting up prayer and worship meetings and outreach to their unbelieving neighbours.

This was a dramatic way for a man to learn about the value of a ministry of prayer. I think I learned a little bit more of this in the Covid pandemic, when meeting was so much harder, shepherding was so much harder and knowing how people were truly doing was so much harder. Yet it really did feel as if "the prayers of God's people [called] down blessing on the work". It was

38 Quoted in Geraldine Taylor, *The Life Changing Story of J.O. Fraser* (OMF International, 1998), p. 52.

wonderful. I'm not sure if that has left a permanent legacy of committed prayer in our church or not, but it did persuade me experientially of what I always knew in my head. Mine is meant to be a ministry of prayer as well as a ministry of the word.

Brothers and sisters, people support our work so that we might have time to meet deeply with Jesus ourselves, to contemplate him and, also, so that we might have more time to pray. This is a great privilege. Newton, once again, puts it memorably and wonderfully:

> The chief means for attaining wisdom are the holy Scriptures and prayer. The one is a fountain of living water, the other a bucket with which we are to draw.[39]

We have been asked by our churches to spend lots of time with God. What a gift!

---

39 John Newton, *The Works of John Newton*, Vol. 1, p. 91.

Interlude

This is not a chapter—more of an interruption. It is here because I am writing a lopsided book about the privileges of ministry. I am telling myself (and inviting you) to dwell upon the joys and sweetness of ministry and not just the sorrows and bitter elements—but I do want to briefly acknowledge that as well as addressing our hearts—how we *see* our ministry—there are some other very practical things we can *do* to keep ourselves encouraged.

I've found that people have started to ask me, "How have you kept going in ministry for the past 25 years?" I think this means I'm getting old! After stumbling through a vague response the first couple of times I was asked this, I took some time to form a more considered answer.

Now, I am telling people that four things have been really helpful:

1. Guarding my heart
2. Having proper friendships
3. Making sure I rest
4. Getting equipped where I am lacking

Most of this book has been concerned with the first of those. This interlude is a brief comment on the other three, because they all make a significant difference in enabling us to keep going (and how we feel as we keep going).

Friendships

Many years ago, I had a conversation with an older pastor who observed, "I've never really kept up with many friends. All my time has gone to ministry and family. There's never been any left for friends spread all over the country." I recall at the time thinking, "Hmm, that doesn't sound very healthy. I don't want to be like that." Of course, with a little more age and a little less self-confidence I realise that it's harder to not be like that than I thought it would be. Yet proper friendships are a wonderful means of grace to us. To have some friends—perhaps especially those who are in ministry and really "get it" and with whom you can meet up to cry, rejoice, lament and laugh at yourself—is a precious gift.

As we saw back in chapter 1, in one of his less encouraging passages Charles Bridges observes:

> A distant view of the ministry is generally very different from what is found when we are actually

> engaged in it. The young soldier, who has never seen an enemy, may form some general notions of what is before him; but his ideas will be much more lively and diversified when he comes upon the field of battle. If the Lord was to show us the whole beforehand, who that has a sense of his own insufficiency and weakness, would venture to engage?[40]

I imagine that if you've been in ministry for any length of time, you can recognise the truth here. When we enter ministry, it turns out to be a lot more complicated than we thought it would be. Yet I take it that if you've got this far in the book, you are someone who wants to keep going, despite the hard days and the heartache, and to minister joyfully. We all need help with that; it's not something that we can do alone. So we need real friends, and it is worth making the effort to have them.

I have one ministry friend who lived in London for many years, serving at another church, but has now moved hundreds of miles away. Once a term he comes to London for 36 hours to catch up one to one with a few London-based friends. That puts friendship on a plate for me, but I'm always struck that he thinks it's well worth the effort to catch up with old friends in ministry. I think most of our catch-ups consist of comparing notes of things that have encouraged us, turning to the (sometimes longer) list of things that are discouraging us, and praying. We also spend some of our time laughing at one another's foibles and failings. There is something wonderfully helpful about pouring

40 Charles Bridges, *The Christian Ministry,* p. 105.

out frustrations and letting someone you trust say to you, "Well, don't you expect this kind of thing? Jesus promises us troubles and joys."

This is also why I go to more pastors' conferences than is probably necessary. If I'm honest, the chief motivation is not the content of the plenary sessions or seminars—it's seeing people. It's a very natural meeting-point to catch up with ministry friends. One delight of getting older is that the hints of competition which were perhaps there when we were younger men have all faded. These days, we're grateful to still be going on in our faith and our ministry, still be married and still be rejoicing in our salvation.

I think that it's only with these kinds of in-person meetings in place that phone calls and phone messages are effective. Having physically laughed and prayed with someone makes it far easier to send a quick message: "Please pray for the meeting I have today because..." or "Can you pray for my son/daughter, who is facing..." and so on.

Personally, I have benefited enormously from friends within the church where I minister. You can't share everything that is burdening you with a congregation member, unlike with a peer in another church, but people within your own church *see* you. They can tell when you're not on good form, they can pointedly (or if needed, forcefully) ask you about the time you've taken off, and they can lift your mood before you recognise that you need it lifting. All of us need friends in our church. We are not to be wiser than the Scriptures: "Encourage one another daily, as long as it is called

'Today', so that none of you may be hardened by sin's deceitfulness" (Hebrews 3:13). Don't be deceived into thinking this applies to your church's congregation but not to its ministers.

In the language of 1 Peter 5, we are shepherds, but we must never forget that we are sheep too—also prone to wander, sometimes into discouragement. Friendship can help provide the shepherding that we need.

Rest

Sometimes the most godly thing we can do is go to bed. At other times, the shortest route to godly behaviour is a day off. At still other times, the most significant factor in restoring joy to our ministry is time away. In the regular run of ministry weeks, we need to find a sabbath; it's no good telling the church family to trust God and rely on him but failing to do so ourselves.

I know, I know—there are some seasons which are crazy, and it's just not possible. Yet those should not be the norm, and when they come, there needs to be some time of compensation afterwards. I'm struck that after the disciples return from their first mission trip, having experienced the wonder of God providing for them (taking no bread, bag or money) and the excitement of preaching, casting out demons and healing, Jesus says, "Come with me by yourselves to a quiet place and rest" (Mark 6:31). They have to wait a little longer for it than planned, while Jesus feeds the 5,000, but it does come.

There is something to learn here. After intense periods of ministry, we need to "come away ... and rest".

I recall being told off one year in my annual appraisal for not taking sufficient rest. It was pointed out that my pattern had become to get to the "end of the year" (in our rhythm that's August, when people take their summer breaks) with my tank down to 20% energy and then have a restorative break and come back in September at 90%. But then the following year, I'd get to the end of July at 15% but return in September at 85%. The following year it would be 10% and 80%. I might have quibbled with the numbers, but I couldn't argue with the reality being pointed out. Something had to change; I had to pace myself during the year so that I didn't end it quite so exhausted.

I think I've observed in others that this pattern can be kept up for a surprisingly long time, but then one unexpected, and perhaps not even particularly major, issue becomes the final straw which leads to burnout or a resignation or (worst of all) a significant moral failure.

You might be reading this thinking that there just aren't enough fellow workers at your church to get everything done. There's a voice in your head saying, "If I don't do what's needed, it will not happen". Well, then maybe it can't happen. And that's okay. The Lord can build his church. He doesn't require you to burn out in order for it to happen. I do think that it becomes easier as we age in ministry to say no and let some things drop—to become better at doing some things passably in order for the most important things to get done well.

My sense is that in the UK more churches offer sabbaticals than people take them up. In the US, the data suggests that only 58% of evangelical church leaders have taken one.[41] My encouragement is: take it. While it *always* feels that planning to take that time is too arduous a challenge, I have *never* met a minister who has taken a sabbatical and said that they regretted it. It is a rich blessing.

Getting Equipped

Sometimes we can be burying ourselves because we can't see a solution or becoming discouraged because we have a weakness that is never addressed. It's much better to take some time to get equipped for an aspect of church ministry than to spend years being burdened by the consequences of never doing so.

In my case, I think that I received a very good theological education, but no one really taught me how to run teams, manage staff or adjust to a growing organisation. So perhaps it shouldn't surprise me that the closest that I came to resigning was when I sat back and thought to myself that the church had outgrown my ability to lead it. I shared this with a few of our elders, and their sensible response was "Why don't we help you improve your ability to lead?"

I had been able to see only two options: carry on miserably or resign. The fact that there was a third—to grow in competence—had honestly not occurred to me. So I sought out people who could actually help me think through how to become better in those areas—how to adjust how church was running. I spent a couple

41 https://www.nae.org/surveys/evangelical-leaders-sabbaticals/ (accessed 6 March 2026).

of months one summer meeting up with leaders of comparably sized London churches. Most of them I didn't know, so I had to "cold-mail" them. Yet most were delighted to meet up. It turned out that all of us recognised that we could benefit from chatting through size dynamics with other church leaders. It was really encouraging for me, as well as equipping me, to find that others had the same challenges as me and to observe how they approached them.

Sometimes we can escape a frustrating period of ministry simply by finding the right advice. It has to be from someone who is willing to take the time to really engage with you, as opposed to projecting their life onto yours. But shrewd advice from people with experience and expertise is priceless. I suspect that too often we stumble on when there are resources at hand that can help.

Another way in which I have personally greatly benefited from is in deliberately pursuing further study. One friend describes a minister's initial theological education as loading up a camel for three or four years and then sending it off into the desert with a cheery "good luck". We can be very poor at further training. I am not very disciplined, and so, to keep reading theologically, I have to sign up for book groups or short courses. If your church is supportive, further assessed study is a great way to be chivvied into further reading and writing. Of course it takes time away from church, but you're doing it so that you can minister to your church more effectively and deeply. You may well not be able to draw a direct line between your study and the benefit to your church, but indirectly it will be good for the flock which you have been called to shepherd.

All of us are different and will vary in what support, input and training will benefit our ministry most. But I'm confident that all of us need to find one or two watering-holes in the desert so that we don't run dry.

So, as we finish this not-a-real-chapter interlude and before we return to the privileges and joys of ministry, take a moment to ask yourself:

- Who are the friends who encourage me? Is there anything I need to do to press into those friendships more?
- Does my family and my church family think that I am in a healthy pattern of work and rest—weekly, annually, and more long-term? Does anything need to change?
- What are the watering holes where I go to keep learning and to get equipped?

Chapter 5

Suffering for the Name

Around a decade ago, a guy joined our church staff team after theological college. He was brilliant. He was godly and able and hugely enjoyable to work with, and he was one of the best young preachers I've known. His handling of the biblical text and his perceptive applications of it into real life were exceptional. Apart, that is, from one series. A few years into his time with us, he began a series in 2 Corinthians. It just didn't click. He stumbled over the exegesis and didn't connect with the congregation. We talked about it, and I gave him lots of help in the week, but come Sunday, each time it would fall flat. I ended up taking the series from him. When he returned to the pulpit in another Bible book, he was, once again, on top form. Neither of us could quite work out why his series on 2 Corinthians was so bad compared to his normal preaching.

Several years later, he had moved on to lead another church, and we happened to catch up. And he said to me, "Do you remember that stinker of a series I preached in 2 Corinthians?" I commented that I did, and that it was bizarre that we couldn't work out what was going on at the time. He responded, "I've worked it out since then—what the problem was. I didn't want 2 Corinthians to be true. I didn't want God's strength to require my weakness."

I didn't want it to be true. That is profound self-awareness and honesty. My younger friend was brilliant in so many ways, but he had never suffered. He wanted to be an excellent pastor but didn't want to endure trials. Years later, when he had experienced emotional and medical trauma, he grew to love 2 Corinthians. It became precious to him, as it is for so many of us in ministry. Personally, I have developed a habit of reading slowly through that letter in January every year—partly because that's the beginning of the year and partly because in the UK it's cold and dark in January, and so it's easy to feel flat. At the start of the year, I need my expectations of Christian ministry to be reset biblically, and 2 Corinthians is the place to do that.

However, while the message of strength in weakness does us good, the question remains: is it really a *privilege* to suffer for Christ? The apostles certainly thought so:

> The apostles left the Sanhedrin, *rejoicing* because they had been counted worthy of suffering disgrace for the Name. (Acts 5:41)

Why did they rejoice? Because they knew that their suffering for Jesus meant that they were the real deal—that they were genuinely disciples who were ministering the gospel of Jesus truly. Suffering as you minister is not an indicator that something is wrong with your ministry. Rather it is the normal New Testament pattern. It reveals that you are following in the pattern of Jesus. After Jesus meets Paul on the road to Damascus, the Lord tells Ananias that "I will show him how much he must suffer for the sake of my name" (Acts 9:16). Of course Paul must suffer for the name of Jesus. That's what apostles do. It's a badge of authenticity. So Paul would later write from prison:

> Now I rejoice in what I am suffering for you, and I fill up in my flesh what is still lacking in regard to Christ's afflictions, for the sake of his body, which is the church. (Colossians 1:24)

There is, of course, nothing lacking in Christ's redemptive suffering. The main thrust of that whole letter is that Christ is all you need! But in two parallel phrases—"what I am suffering for you" and "I fill up in my flesh what is still lacking in regard to Christ's afflictions"—Paul describes his ministry of taking the gospel of Jesus out across the world. It's hard work, and it's painful work! His goal is to present believers mature in Christ: "To this end I strenuously contend with all the energy Christ so powerfully works in me" (v 29).

This is not about apostolic ministry so much as about pastoral ministry. There are a lot of unique things about the apostles, but suffering for the gospel is not one of them. Paul told the believers in Philippi:

> For it has been granted to you on behalf of Christ not only to believe in him, but also to suffer for him. (Philippians 1:29)

The believers were "granted" or "gifted" (*charizomai*, the same word as for spiritual gifts) this privilege: to suffer for Christ. We're not to think, "I don't want that gift... can I politely exchange it for something else, like I do occasionally with some Christmas presents?" This gift enables us to draw closer to Christ, to have a life shaped like his: a ministry which follows the contours of his.

Similarly, Paul wrote in his second letter to Timothy:

> So do not be ashamed of the testimony about our Lord or of me his prisoner. Rather, join with me in suffering for the gospel, by the power of God.
>
> (2 Timothy 1:8)

It is somewhat of a theme verse for the letter. And in significant contrast, "Demas, because he loved this world, has deserted me" (4:10). We don't know the details, but it's a telling summary of why one colleague of Paul's had deserted him: "he loved this world" and was unwilling to join in suffering. I think we can take from that the implication that if we *are* willing to endure suffering, then we are being weaned away from a love for the world. So, be encouraged.

Genuine gospel ministry is hard. It is exhausting (though I will add a caution to that blunt statement below).

Knowing Death and Resurrection

I mentioned in the previous chapter that, when I was a young Christian, my favourite verse (and the key to accessing all my data) was Philippians 3:8: "I consider everything a loss because of the surpassing worth of knowing Christ Jesus my Lord". Yet, while I always loved that verse, I was never entirely sure what to do with verses 10-11:

> I want to know Christ—yes, to know the power of his resurrection and participation in his sufferings, becoming like him in his death, and so, somehow, attaining to the resurrection from the dead.

I could see that following Jesus could involve death and resurrection. And, to be honest, I was keener on the resurrection power than I was on participation in sufferings. Then I realised that these are not sequential experiences; they are simultaneous ones. It's quite normal to experience death and resurrection *at the same time*. Paul writes of this experience in 2 Corinthians:

> We always carry around in our body the death of Jesus, so that the life of Jesus may also be revealed in our body. For we who are alive are always being given over to death for Jesus' sake, so that his life may also be revealed in our mortal body. (4:10-11)

Paul "always" carried death *and* resurrection life with him. That is normal ministry, and experiencing this reveals that you are a genuine minister, pointing people towards the Lord Jesus Christ. In a bracing passage that I sometimes need to reread, the medieval writer Thomas à Kempis wrote:

> Jesus has always many who love his heavenly kingdom, but few who bear his cross. He has many who desire consolation, but few who care for trial. He

> finds many to share his table, but few to take part in his fasting. All desire to be happy with him; few wish to suffer anything for him. Many follow him to the breaking of bread, but few to the drinking of the chalice of His passion. Many revere his miracles; few approach the shame of the cross. Many love him as long as they encounter no hardship; many praise and bless him, so long as they receive some comfort from him. But if Jesus hides himself and leaves them for a while, they fall either into complaints or into deep dejection.[42]

I find that I benefit from self-catechism said out loud—so sometimes I'll ask myself some blunt questions and answers:

1. Matt, do you want to be like Christ in your ministry? *Then ministry cannot be cost-free and easy.*
2. Matt, do you want to see others grow more like Christ? *Then you cannot teach and model a life without cost.*
3. Matt, do you want to know Christ better, to love him and adore him more? *Then you must participate in his sufferings and become like him*

---

42 Thomas à Kempis, *The Imitation of Christ*, Book II, Chapter XI, titled "Of the Fewness of Those Who Love the Cross of Jesus". swartzentrover.com+2documentacatholicaomnia.eu+2 (accessed 3 March 2026). To clarify, the Christian should read this as one who is already justified and accepted by God. It is not clear that Thomas à Kempis had that unconditional grace in view and his *Imitation* gives the impression that salvation is through imitation of Christ rather than faith in him.

> *in his death, while also experiencing the power of his resurrection life.*

There is great encouragement in knowing that we enter the kingdom of God through hardships. Certainly, Paul thought so. I'm always struck by this brief account in Acts 14:

> Then some Jews came from Antioch and Iconium and won the crowd over. They stoned Paul and dragged him outside the city, thinking he was dead. But after the disciples had gathered around him, he got up and went back into the city. The next day he and Barnabas left for Derbe. They preached the gospel in that city and won a large number of disciples. Then they returned to Lystra, Iconium and Antioch, strengthening the disciples and encouraging them to remain true to the faith. (v 19-22a)

Luke's succinct account raises all sorts of questions. What state was Paul in as he lay outside the city of Lystra, which meant the Jews thought he was dead? How long after this stoning did he and Barnabas return to Lystra? That was brave, given that Paul had almost died there—yet he thought it so important to strengthen the young believers that he risked his life again. But what was the message he needed them to hear, to strengthen and encourage them?

> We must go through many hardships to enter the kingdom of God. (v 22b)

Why is this encouraging? Because it means that life has not gone wrong when hardships come. Your ministry is not failing when tribulations arrive. This is normal for believers on their way to the consummated kingdom of God in glory.

When suffering and hardship come, sometimes the heart of our discouragement is that we didn't truly expect this. Somewhere deep down we functionally believe that if we serve Christ, then things will go smoothly; that we are competent people and can manage ministry effectively; that ministry should become easier as we grow in competency or experience. We know that's not true biblically—yet somehow this "old self" thinking persists. I've chewed over this observation of Newton's many times:

> Most of our perplexities arise from an undue, though perhaps unperceived, attachment to self. Either we have some scheme of our own too closely connected with our general view of serving the Lord or lay some stress upon our own management, which, though we suspect it fails us, we cannot entirely help trusting to.[43]

Newton certainly nails me. Discouragement sometimes comes because I had a brilliant idea for church that fell flat, or I couldn't prevent that couple leaving when they fell out with some others, or because ministry turns out to be, quite simply, much harder than I imagined. Well, what did I expect? I really should know that "we must go through many hardships to enter the kingdom of God".

43 John Newton, *The Works of John Newton,* Vol. 1, p. 338.

On Burning Out or Glooming Out

We need to pause here to notice the possibility of making two overlapping mistakes. While recognising that Paul always carried in his body the death of Christ *and* his resurrection life, and that gospel ministry is tiring, we also need to recognise and balance this with the command to rest. We must first avoid burning out, and second avoid glooming out. (I've made that phrase up.)

In April 2021, when I hit the wall and my elders made me to take time off to recover, I had a degree of burnout. With hindsight, it was caused by a combination of things. I had some unhealthy long-term patterns of work and had never really emerged from church-planting mode, even after 20 years. My parents had both died in short succession. Navigating the church through Covid was hard work. The final straw was becoming embroiled in trying to help another church with a complicated leadership mess. I had pushed myself too hard for too long and had failed to take seriously the biblical command to rest. I had not got right the basics of exercising, eating sensibly and investing time in friendships.

The elders kindly sent me for some grief counselling. The most helpful line in those conversations occurred a couple of meetings in, when the counsellor asked me, "What do you understand by 'self-care', and how is it different from selfishness?" I floundered away as I tried to answer, and then I admitted that I wasn't sure. That was revealing! His succinct response was that selfishness is taking inappropriately high levels of time off to please yourself. Self-care is taking divinely ordered time off to honour God and serve others.

That helped me greatly. In my head I had assumed that self-care equals selfishness (which no pastor seeks to pursue). I came to realise that a *lack* of self-care equals disobedience and an inability to serve healthily. Here is the take-home: *self-care, carefully defined, is a good thing.*

Ministry is a vocation and not just a job. In part, this is why many of us find it so fulfilling. In any church there is always an endless list of useful things to do and people to meet. Yet God has given us parameters of rest and wise patterns of life. We are, like Paul, to "strenuously contend with all the energy Christ so powerfully works in [us]" (Colossians 1:29) so that we might present believers mature in Christ. But this must not be done at the expense of forgetting our fragility and our limitations—in other words, our creaturely humanity.[44]

The second danger is that we might "gloom out". Glooming out happens when we functionally only read half of the texts from Paul that we looked at earlier:

> I want to know Christ: yes, to know ~~the power of his resurrection and~~ participation in his sufferings, becoming like him in his death. (Philippians 3:10)

> We always carry around in our body the death of Jesus, ~~so that the life of Jesus may also be revealed in~~

44 *Zeal Without Burnout* by Christopher Ash (The Good Book Company, 2016) and *Resilient Ministry* by Bob Burns, Tasha Chapman and Donald C. Guthrie (IVP USA, 2013) are both profoundly helpful on this topic.

> ~~our body~~. For we ~~who are alive~~ are always being given over to death for Jesus' sake, ~~so that his life may also be revealed~~ in our mortal body.
>
> (2 Corinthians 4:10-11)

That is, it's possible that we focus...

- on following the pattern of suffering, while forgetting that God is also at work in us.
- on strenuously labouring, while forgetting the resurrection power within us.
- upon our weaknesses, while forgetting that "the joy of the LORD is [our] strength" (Nehemiah 8:10).

In other words, we forget that, in Newton's words from chapter 1, ministry is not only sorrowful and bitter but also a joy that is full of sweetness. To quote him again, yes, the task is urgent, but the Lord provides us with what we need for the task if we carry it out in his way and look to him. We need...

> a heart impressed with some real abiding sense of the love of God, the worth of souls, the shortness of time, and the importance of eternity. Without this turn of mind, though a man should spend sixteen hours every day in his study, he may be a mere trifler.[45]

You and I need to spend enough time in the Scriptures and in prayer so that our hearts are impressed with

45 John Newton, *The Works of John Newton*, Vol. 1, p. 91.

these truths and can sustain us in precious eternal work that we get to do. "Sustainable sacrifice" is a tricky sweet spot to find. Some of us may sacrifice in a manner which is okay when we start but is not sustainable in the long term. Others of us may have a ministry all about sustainability, but it's hard to see the sacrifice. The models that we had in our formation are often key in shaping this. Commonly it requires accountability and good friends to help us see how we're doing in this regard.

What If I'm Not Suffering for Christ?

In my early years in ministry, I think I lived with a slight lingering sense of guilt. I worked hard and gave myself to serving, but, in truth, I loved it and couldn't really see where the suffering was. I could look at peers of mine who were enduring far greater trials than me and feel somewhat embarrassed by my relative ease. I read of, and prayed for, the persecuted church elsewhere in the world and sometimes felt bewildered by the discrepancy between their trials and mine. Sure, some people were rude about my beliefs, but it wasn't quite the same as the apostles being arrested or believers being martyred. Yet I came to realise that denying self and taking up my cross was a reality in my own life—and it probably is in yours, too, even if you are not suffering greatly. Let me suggest some ways that you may well be "suffering disgrace for the name"...

Suffering a Loss of Status

When I was a teacher, people understood what I did and respected (or even loved) what I did. Now when I tell people I'm a pastor, I can sense the discomfort. It may vary in different parts of the world, but certainly, in the UK, in 2025, there is no great respect for pastors. Those I meet who are socially smooth generally recover sufficient poise (after their initial horror at being stuck in conversation with a pastor) to ask, "What do you *do* all day long?"

Similarly, I recently had a great couple of days with some old friends from university days to mark 30 years since we had graduated. I was a little taken aback by the blunt question: "Matt, are you still in the same church where you've been for 25 years? What happened to your ambition?"

It's not a big deal. But no one is impressed by pastors. That is, no one apart from the living God.

John Owen reminds us that we should never be ashamed of the ministry because God is not ashamed of us:

> Would it be a shame for the great and glorious God to own poor, despised, condemned and persecuted ones? No, God is not ashamed to be called their God ... O that we could persuade our hearts in every duty that belongs to us that Jesus Christ stands by and says, "I am not ashamed of you!" God stands by and says, "I am not ashamed of being known as your God!" Isn't this a great encouragement?[46]

---

46 John Owen, *Gospel Ministry*, p. 27.

Enduring Criticism

Criticism comes when you lead. I was struck recently when reading a largely secular book on leadership by Edwin Friedman in which he suggested that someone is always seeking to sabotage your leadership.[47] He's not saying that the sabotage is necessarily deliberate or intentional—sometimes it is quite unwitting. Clearly, it can vary in strength and complexity. Yet, it comes with the role. I have some friends who have been driven out of churches because the criticism went on for so long and was so forceful that they couldn't carry on. I'm sure I'd have been the same. I have other friends who have had to deal with years of exaggerated official complaints made against them to denominational officials, not really over behaviour but due to theological disagreement.

Criticism is exhausting. I think the times I find hardest are when people are passionately certain that I've handled a complicated pastoral issue wrongly, but they don't know all the information and I'm not allowed to share the information (and nor would it be appropriate). It's painful when you can't really explain.

A whole stack of criticism falls into the bucket of low-level disagreement. On this, the simple advice I was given decades ago remains profoundly helpful: there are three "E"s of criticism—expect it, evaluate it and endure it.

- *Expect it*, for it will inevitably come. There is a reason why New Testament epistles are loaded

47 Edwin Friedman, *A Failure of Nerve* (Church Publishing New York, 2017). The theme of sabotage runs throughout the Introduction.

with the very simple-to-understand-yet-hard-to-do command: bear with one another, forgive one another and be patient with one another (for example, Ephesians 4:2, 32).

- *Evaluate it*, because often people have a complaint or raise an issue which is true. There is much to be learned from criticism. It's also often the case that people will shout a complaint at 10/10 volume, but when you evaluate their issue, you'll find that while they are correct, it probably only warrants a 3/10 level.
- *Endure it*. When we're criticised, it's not as if we're being shot at or physically beaten, but there have certainly been times when I have felt beaten up at the end of a conversation—days when I've come home, sat on the kitchen floor and cried. My wife tends to remind me of some simple truths on these occasions:

  > For it is commendable if someone bears up under the pain of unjust suffering because they are conscious of God. But how is it to your credit if you receive a beating for doing wrong and endure it? But if you suffer for doing good and you endure it, this is commendable before God.
  > (1 Peter 2:19-20)

Be encouraged: it is a commendable thing in God's sight when we endure unjust criticism.

Constant Anxiety

To return to 2 Corinthians, after Paul lists some of his sufferings—floggings, exposure to death, shipwreck, often without food or sleep—it is striking that he concludes the list with this:

> Besides everything else, I face daily the pressure of my concern for all the churches. Who is weak, and I do not feel weak? Who is led into sin, and I do not inwardly burn? (2 Corinthians 11:28-29)

A pastor's heart is a broken heart. It's impossible to love and care for people without feeling anxious about their wellbeing—without being distraught at a marriage collapsing, a baby dying or a believer wobbling. Who of us has not lain awake all night, worrying whether Peter will keep going in the faith, whether Jane, in her anger, will persuade others that I've acted unreasonably, or whether Zack will come back to church?

We can't know for certain, but it may be that Paul positions this "pressure" at the end of the list as a climax. It clearly lacks the intense agony of being flogged, but this was for him a "daily ... pressure"—and sometimes this is what can grind us down. There are seasons in church life when there are just so many individuals and families in pain or facing difficult decisions (or making foolish ones). In my experience, there never seems to be an even spread of issues—they seem to come in clusters.

It is certainly no accident that it is after his list of sufferings—ministry and personal—that Paul famously says in chapter 12:

> [God] said to me, "My grace is sufficient for you, for my power is made perfect in weakness." Therefore I will boast all the more gladly about my weaknesses, so that Christ's power may rest on me. (v 9)

There it is again: Paul wants Christ's power to rest on him. He wants to know resurrection power alongside participation in sufferings. In the end, the privilege of suffering is that of being drawn into closer communion with Jesus. As Richard Sibbes puts it, our afflictions are God's medicine:

> Physicians, though they put their patients to much pain, will not destroy nature, but raise it up by degrees. Surgeons will lance and cut, but not dismember.[48]

The Lord uses our sufferings to cure us from certain sinful patterns. Similarly, Charles Spurgeon piles up the metaphors in a wonderful sermon on affliction:

> They who dive in the sea of affliction bring up rare pearls ... When cast into the cellars of affliction, remember that the great king keeps his wine there; the best and most mature wines.[49]

It is a privilege to suffer in ministry. We meet Christ there. He transforms us there. Be encouraged if personally you're in the sea or the cellars of affliction right now. The New Testament expects us to spend some time there. And be encouraged if, in your pastoral

---

48 Richard Sibbes, *The Bruised Reed* (Banner of Truth, 1998), p. 7.
49 Charles Spurgeon, "Sermon 619", *The Metropolitan Tabernacle Pulpit*, 1865.

ministry, you are going into the sea and the cellars with other people right now, to share their pain and sit with them. It is exhausting but also a privilege. I think of babies that I've buried when, apart from the parents, I was the only person to meet them when alive. I think of times at the bedside of people dying, seeing them cling tightly to Christ in their final hours. I think of times when people have shared the details of the secret shames of their lives. These are burdensome but also an honour. What a privilege to be able to observe the deep work of God that takes place in people's lives when they are in the sea or cellars.

So, don't despise the suffering or the cost. (I write this to myself.) In them, the Lord is affirming the reality of our faith. He is weaning us off this world. He is transforming us into the likeness of his Son. He is directing our gaze to heaven.

And there is a crown awaiting us there, as we'll see in chapter 7. Before we get to that, though, 1 Peter 5 has one more privilege to lay before us.

Chapter 6

Examples for the Flock

A decade ago, we had to say goodbye to a little girl whom we thought we had adopted.

She came to us not long after she was born, from a very messy and distressing background. It was a crisis fostering placement, but we were led to believe that the legal formalities would inevitably follow. The next twelve months were, without a doubt, the happiest year of my life. We became a family of four, and she brought immeasurable joy and laughter to our house and wider family.

Then, at the final adoption hearing, the judge decided that she would be better off with a distant relative overseas.

The decision was a monumental shock to us, the adoption agency and social services. Saying goodbye to a one-year-old who we felt was our daughter, whom we deeply loved and whom we had raised from birth, was brutal. It broke us. My wife, my son and I all collapsed at different points.

During that time an older minister wrote a lovely note to me, full of rich, consoling wisdom. But the section in it that struck me most was where he said:

> You are about to experience the strange privilege of suffering in front of the whole congregation. You would never have chosen this, but I doubt there will be another stage in your ministry when you will teach people as much as you will do now. This will underline all your ministry thus far and provide many opportunities in the future. It's very hard processing this in the public eye as pastor, but it is, in a strange way, a privilege to do so.

In the context of our friendship (and a far longer letter), those words were, perhaps surprisingly, not at all burdensome. I read them as a helpful observation and found them strangely encouraging. We could still be useful, even as we collapsed, because we could set an example. I realised, more deeply than before, that pastors and their families are always living as examples in front of their churches. Not just in times of obvious trial but also in the humdrum seasons of life. There is a strange privilege in that. We can make a transforming difference to others by the way we live our lives.

It's a concern that Peter highlights in our familiar passage:

> Be shepherds of God's flock that is under your care ... being examples to the flock. (1 Peter 5:2-3)

That's the command to pastors—be an example. I think Peter means it as an encouragement, not just a command.

I see it as a privilege. And so I'm conscious of two likely objections: I'*m not sure that it's a privilege to be an example* and *I'm not sure that I am always a great example.*

Why Is Setting an Example a Privilege?

Being an example is very much a part of the "noble task" that Paul commends to Timothy (1 Timothy 3:1). The verses that follow this description of pastoring are all about the character that we are to model (v 2-7). Elsewhere Paul frequently offers himself up as an example or model (*tupos*—it's the same word as in 1 Peter 5:3):

> Join together in following my example, brothers and sisters, and just as you have us as a *model*, keep your eyes on those who live as we do. (Philippians 3:17)

> We did this, not because we do not have the right to such help, but in order to offer ourselves as a *model* for you to imitate. (2 Thessalonians 3:9)

And he commands both Titus and Timothy to do the same—to be an example for the churches they lead:

> In everything set them an *example* by doing what is good. In your teaching show integrity, seriousness... (Titus 2:7)

> Set an *example* for the believers in speech, in conduct, in love, in faith, in purity. (1 Timothy 4:12)

William Mounce comments on *tupos*: "The word picture it paints is not so much that Timothy is an example that others can emulate but that he is a mould that should be pressed into the lives of others so that they attain the same shape."[50] That's a striking image—one that reminds us of the responsibility that we have in ministry and the way we can do good or harm. What shape do we impress upon others? To what extent is it the outline of the fruit of the Spirit?

Having pastored the same church for 25 years, from when it began as a church plant, for good and bad I need to accept that I must have had a significant impact in pressing the church family into a certain shape or mould. I should not be naïve about that. Whenever I'm encouraged to do a personality test (Myers Briggs, Hogan, VIA and so on), I find that I am way above average in introspection and self-criticism. I naturally find it very hard to think that I can be a positive example. Yet occasionally, *even I* get letters and cards thanking me for the example I've set. To my surprise, some people thank God for the model of Christian living that my wife and I have provided.

What an enormous difference we can make in people's lives through the example that we offer. In some ways it is an overwhelming responsibility—and yet what a privilege and honour that the Lord has given us. Yes—we get to make a difference!

Sir Gareth Southgate was manager of the England football team. He received his knighthood not only for improving the results of the national team but crucially also for changing the culture of the team and the mood around them. He took an unhappy group

---

50 William Mounce, *The Pastoral Epistles*, Word Biblical Commentary, Vol. 46 (Zondervan, 2017), p. 259.

with potential and created a confident team that clearly enjoyed playing for the nation and for him. He has spoken eloquently and frequently about the need for role models to build resilience and mould the character of the next generation. One of his driving philosophies was "We have to show young men that character is more important than status."[51]

Southgate wanted to mould a generation of footballers. You and I get to mould a generation of church members. And much of it happens through our example. To rephrase Southgate, each of us can say, "I get to show other Christians that Christ, and Christ-likeness, are more important than anything the world can offer".

I'm Not Sure I'm Setting a Great Example

If this objection is currently nudging insistently at you, well, it may well be true! But Paul tells Timothy to show people progress:

> Don't let anyone look down on you because you are young, but set an example for the believers in speech, in conduct, in love, in faith and in purity. Until I come, devote yourself to the public reading of Scripture, to preaching and to teaching. Do not neglect your gift, which was given you through prophecy when the body of elders laid their hands on you. Be diligent in these matters; give yourself wholly to them, *so that everyone may see your progress.* Watch

51 Quote from the Richard Dimbleby Lecture, Thursday 20th March 2025, https://www.bbc.co.uk/programmes/m00293l5 (accessed 3 March 2026).

> your life and doctrine closely. Persevere in them, because if you do, you will save both yourself and your hearers. (1 Timothy 4:12-16)

It's often said, but bears repeating, that the Lord doesn't expect perfection but progress. We touched on this briefly in chapter 4: sometimes we aim too high and get discouraged. But progress is always achievable! It also puts us in good company; Luke records that Jesus "*made progress* in wisdom and stature, and in favour with God and man" (Luke 2:52).[52] Most scholars suggest Timothy was in his mid-30s and younger than many in the congregation at Ephesus. Perhaps he wasn't all they wanted him to be. Maybe there were others with a more rounded Christian character. But he could still *make progress* as an example for them. After all, making progress was an example that every member of his congregation, however far along in maturity, could follow.

And Paul describes the nature of the progress Timothy was to aim for in the rest of that paragraph:

1. Lifestyle

> Set an example for the believers in speech, in conduct, in love, in faith and in purity.

The first two traits are more obviously seen in public, while the latter three are more private. However, we should expect that those inner qualities (or lack of them) will eventually be seen in public too. We would

52 Here Luke is using the verbal form of the noun for progress (*prokopé*).

expect progress in love, faith and purity to be seen in speech and conduct.

It is increasingly the case that when I encourage a young man or woman to consider vocational ministry, their response is that they're not sure their character is up to the mark. Of course, that may be true, and it would therefore be inappropriate for them to enter ministry currently. However, for others it is the case that they have an overly tender conscience. For those in this group, I sometimes offer the encouragement that being in ministry can itself drive godliness. For myself, there are times when temptation rears its head, and it is not my love for Christ that prevents me from indulging so much as an awareness of how discouraged others would be if they knew I had stumbled. It is the fear of negatively affecting others that prevents my conduct from falling.

I would prefer love for Christ to always be my governing motivation. But I console myself that the Lord can use different means to encourage godliness. As is often the case, I'm helped by John Newton's honesty in confessing something similar:

> Though he [the pastor] knows that communion with God is the highest privilege, he too seldom finds it so; on the contrary, if duty, conscience, and necessity did not compel, he would leave the throne of grace unvisited from day to day. He takes up the Bible, conscious that it is the fountain of life and true comfort; yet perhaps while he is making the reflection, he feels a secret distaste, which causes

> him to lay it down and give his preference to a newspaper.[53]

Sometimes, it is "duty, conscience, and necessity" that push us to spend time with the Lord. A fear of doing something morally daft tethers us. In my better moments, I long to be an encouragement and a model of consistent Christian living. I cannot abide the thought of standing up and preaching as a hypocrite, and that spurs me to maintain godly conduct. I dread the prospect of causing a little one to stumble (Matthew 18:6), and I find that this encourages me to cut off those things that cause me to stumble (v 8). I am grateful that the responsibility of being an example fuels my longing for sanctification. It must not be the only motivation, but sometimes it is knowing my duty to others that drives my behaviour before God, and consequently I arrive in a place of obedience and blessing.

Paul seems to encourage deacons with a similar thought in 1 Timothy 3:13: "Those who have served well gain an excellent standing and great assurance in their faith in Christ Jesus". Those who serve well (defined in v 8-9 in terms of their character, including a clear conscience) are strengthened in their faith and their personal walk with Jesus. There is a virtuous spiral here: serve Christ faithfully, and you'll be strengthened in your faith to serve him ever more faithfully. The task of ministry helps us in this. The fact that we are an example can spur us on in godliness. That's a blessing.

---

53 John Newton, *The Works of John Newton*, Vol. 1, p. 312.

And even (in fact, especially) on our bad days, one area where we can obviously model Christian living to others is in repentance. After I became a Christian, the first person who got hold of me and read the Bible with me was a minister called Tim. I can't remember much of what we studied,[54] but he did instil in me a delight in repentance. In no way did he burden me, the younger man, with his sin—nor did he share anything inappropriate. But, whenever we met, he would tell me something that he had repented of: perhaps being angry with someone or coveting needless goods or gossiping. Then he would display the pleasure of knowing forgiveness and his determination to go again and, by God's grace, make progress in that area.

Tim was a wonderful example to me of someone who was honest about his flaws, who was determined to grow and who rejoiced in God's mercy over a variety of areas of his life. I simply assumed that's what all Christians did. Of course, I was young and perhaps at a more obviously "mouldable" age. But there is a right sense in which the pastor should model that the whole of the Christian life is one of repentance. Without being inappropriate, we should be specific in this. Talking in generalities about repentance is okay, but it's when we ourselves are specific that we can help model repentance over particular sins and hopefully build a culture of honesty. May I ask: when was the last time that you, publicly or in a small group, repented of something specific?

---

54 Sorry, Tim—I remember 1 John and some of John's Gospel... I'm sure they were faithful Bible studies!

2. Handling Scripture

> Until I come, devote yourself to the public reading of Scripture, to preaching and to teaching.

In chapter 3 of this book we thought about the gift that it was to be paid a salary to grow in our understanding of God's word, and I won't repeat that chapter here! But notice that you can encourage your congregation by making progress in your preaching.

Similarly, the saints at church will be encouraged when we stretch our thinking to teach them more deeply. There *is* time to read in ministry—but we never find that time; we have to make it. I remember reading some helpful calculations done by John Piper:

> Suppose you read slowly, like I do—maybe [at] about the same speed that you speak—200 words a minute. If you read [for] fifteen minutes a day for one year (say just before supper, or just before bed), you will read [for] 5,475 minutes in the year. Multiply that by 200 words a minute, and you get 1,095,000 words that you would read in a year. Now an average serious book might have about 360 words per page. So you would have read 3,041 pages in one year. That's ten very substantial books. All in fifteen minutes a day.[55]

Fifteen minutes a day to keep on making theological progress? I can do that. So can you. So can most Christians, so let's be an example to them.

55 John Piper, *When I Don't Desire God* (Crossway, 2004), p. 129.

3. Maintaining Zeal and Persevering

> Do not neglect your gift, which was given you through prophecy when the body of elders laid their hands on you ... Watch your life and doctrine closely. Persevere in them.

Mounce observes that the verb "do not neglect" can be understood as an encouragement to those who are weary and faltering.[56] As we've considered throughout this book, it's very easy to become tired and discouraged. Yet the Lord commands us in Scripture to "never be lacking in zeal" (Romans 12:11). There are certainly points where I need to take my heart in my hands, as Richard Baxter reminds me:

> If it be not your daily business to study your own hearts, and to subdue corruption and to walk with God—if you make not this a work to which you constantly attend, all will go wrong, and you will starve your hearers.[57]

"Study your own hearts ... walk with God" or "all will go wrong". I know that experience. Baxter tends to write in bracing terms, but don't hear that as a rebuke. Ask the Lord to restore your zeal as you walk with him. Ask others to pray for your zeal.

And then, keep going. Persevere. At times we will feel as if we're running. Most of the time, we'll be plodding. And there'll be harder seasons when we are crawling. But we're called to persevere, not to stand still.

In 1907, Archibald Brown had the daunting task of

---

56 William Mounce, *The Pastoral Epistles*, p. 259.

57 Richard Baxter, *The Reformed Pastor*, p. 62.

ministering at the Metropolitan Tabernacle in London. He came on staff alongside Thomas Spurgeon, who had taken over from his father, Charles. That's a tough act of follow! Two years into the task, Brown wrote to the elders and deacons of the church. He wanted to resign:

> Next month I complete two years of service at the Tabernacle, and after much thought and prayer I have been led to the decision not to prolong the same. I can honestly say that "I have done my best." From the commencement however there have been difficulties that I never dreamed of.

Wonderfully, the elders and deacons took their time, prayed and then replied to Brown:

> Satan will weaken God's hosts and steal the heart from the bravest if he can. He will multiply temptations and inducements to surrender; not only our field of service, but our homes and our social circles will yield him arguments to hinder us, at the time when our Lord needs us the most. Will you not hearten us by a new manifestation of prayerful faith and the zeal you have exhibited ever since your early ministry, to do battle more vigorously with the powers of evil? The Master we adore and love is by your side! Your Church is with you! Difficulties of every shape and complexion are but tests of holy courage ... Dear Pastor, accept our affectionate assurance that we believe God has chosen you to stand for him in this mighty war.[58]

---

58 Iain H. Murray, *Archibald G. Brown: Spurgeon's Successor* (Banner of Truth, 2011), ch. 13.

Archibald Brown did indeed carry on.[59]

There will be times when we need our arms held up by others (Exodus 17:8-13). There will also be times when our own zeal will be a great encouragement and example to others. At times, simply putting one foot in front of the other and carrying on in Christian ministry, despite the pressures, despite the discouragements and frustrations, despite the querulous individuals and the exhausting personal circumstances, will be inspiring to others.

Of course, you may not be sure you are actually making progress. I imagine most of us feel like this at times. Well, what do your family and friends think? Would they say you've made progress in your life and doctrine? They may well be better judges than you!

The Tempter and the Helper

As we've previously noted, surely Satan will attack those in ministry more than the average believer. The damage he can do through the fall of a pastor is often much greater than that of a church member. Never be surprised that Satan rages against you and assails you with temptations. He didn't give up on tempting Jesus after the wilderness; Jesus viewed Peter's encouragement to opt out of the cross as satanic, and the encounter in the Garden of Gethsemane was evidently intense. Why would we, his disciples and ministers, expect different treatment from our master?

---

59 Although sadly, ill-health meant that it was only for a further two years.

In fact, perhaps we should find a lack of temptation worrying rather than finding constant temptation discouraging. Samuel Rutherford observed pithily, "There is no temptation like being without temptation."[60] It is perhaps when we become confident about our ability to resist sin that we lose vigilance and are most vulnerable. (Paul certainly thought so—1 Corinthians 10:12.) In this sense, a nervous caution about our progress in godliness is probably a good thing.

Again, I find Newton's honesty an encouragement:

> I want to devote body and soul, every talent, power and faculty, to the service of his cause ... yet I believe the best of the Lord's servants see cause enough to confess, that they are not only unprofitable in comparison of what they want to be, but in many instances unfaithful likewise. They find so many snares, hindrances, and temptations, arising from without, and so much embarrassment from sin which dwells within, that they have more cause for humiliation than self-complacence when they seem most earnest and most useful.[61]

Yet we can be an example in our battle. We can be examples of those who keep going when they stumble. We can be examples in singing of God's grace which pays for our failures, and examples of God's grace which is slowly transforming us. God uses our frailties to keep us reliant on him.

---

60 Quoted by John Newton, *The Works of John Newton,* Vol. 1, p. 180.
61 As above, p. 337.

Apart from the hymn "What Contradictions Meet", which I quoted in chapter 1, the other Newton hymn that is printed out and sits above my desk at home is this one:

I asked the Lord that I might grow
In faith and love and ev'ry grace,
Might more of his salvation know,
And seek more earnestly his face.

'Twas he who taught me thus to pray,
And he, I trust, has answered prayer,
But it has been in such a way
As almost drove me to despair.

I hoped that in some favoured hour
At once he'd answer my request
And, by his love's constraining pow'r,
Subdue my sins and give me rest.

Instead of this, he made me feel
The hidden evils of my heart
And let the angry pow'rs of hell
Assault my soul in ev'ry part.

Yea, more with his own hand he seemed
Intent to aggravate my woe,
Crossed all the fair designs I schemed,
Humbled my heart and laid me low.

"Lord, why is this?" I trembling cried;
"Wilt thou pursue thy worm to death?"
"'Tis in this way," the Lord replied,
"I answer prayer for grace and faith."

"These inward trials I employ
From self and pride to set thee free
And break thy schemes of earthly joy
That thou may'st find thy all in me."

Isn't that often the way? I'm sure I'm not the only one who has stumbled into some time off feeling exhausted and thought, "I'll recover now", only to be hit by family tragedy or a pastoral bomb. I'm sure I'm not the only one who has found themselves praying, "Lord, I think these circumstances are beyond my ability to be godly". But I tend to imagine the Lord's response to my prayer will be, *They are indeed. You had better rely upon me to get you through.*

Surely in this there is another helpful way to be an example to the church family: to be an example of reliance on the Lord to help us in the midst of frailty and trials. Of course there is a balance to be struck—a military friend once advised me, "Don't unsettle the troops too much with your anxieties". But as pastors in ministry, we must be examples of honest Christian living. This is why, for a while now at our church, we have banned the word "fine". It's a very English response to the question "How are you?" It can effectively stand for "<u>F</u>eelings <u>I</u>nside <u>N</u>ot <u>E</u>xpressed". It can prevent us, as those in ministry, from sharing that we are, in truth, "hard-pressed ... but not crushed" (2 Corinthians 4:8). While there are lots of sunny days in ministry, I think that particular combination is one of the situations that I most commonly feel. Yet, I also find that sharing this truth is an encouraging example to others. If I'm only ever willing to share that I'm "fine", even when really I'm not, I'm moulding my church to be the same.

The Example of Service

Let's return to 1 Peter 5 as we close this chapter, as there is one specific way that Peter encourages us to be an example. As shepherds, we are "not [to be] lording it over those entrusted to you" but instead to be "examples to the flock" (v 3).

I have always imagined Peter pausing as he wrote that sentence and dwelling upon the awkward scene recorded in Mark 10, when James and John had asked for the most prominent positions at Jesus' side in glory and when he and the other disciples had responded with indignation, presumably because the two brothers had stolen a march on them. In familiar words, Jesus told his disciples:

> You know that those who are regarded as rulers of the Gentiles lord it over them, and their high officials exercise authority over them. Not so with you. Instead, whoever wants to become great among you must be your servant, and whoever wants to be first must be slave of all. (v 42-44)

We all know this. It's very simple. Worldly greatness is gaining for self—kingdom greatness is giving of self. Worldly greatness is for personal gain; it pulls rank to make life easier. Kingdom greatness is giving of self to help others grow and develop. And pastors are called to be an example of kingdom greatness.

This doesn't mean that we're to do every job in

church until we drop; serving others involves helping them grow and flourish. Equally, though, it doesn't mean only serving in ways we enjoy. Jesus' greatness was in stooping down to serve us, all the way from heaven to the cross. It's a greatness that we are called to follow and to show as an example. Not perfectly, but making progress as an example to the flock, that they may be moulded into Christ-likeness. We get to make a difference through the example that we set. It's a privilege to be able to do so.

Chapter 7

Awaiting the Crown

"When the Chief Shepherd appears, you will receive the crown of glory that will never fade away."
1 Peter 5:4

That is a very precious truth, and I need reminding of it frequently. No matter how hard ministry may feel, it will all be worthwhile. In the simple sentence of Thomas Goodwin:

> Heaven will make amends for all; God will be better to thee than all.[62]

Medals and Crowns

A few years ago, I interviewed the Christian Olympic rower Debbie Flood at an outreach event. She and her crew were five-time world champions at quadruple sculls. They were fully expected to win gold at the Olympics in 2004 but came second. Then in 2008 they

---

62 Ed. Thomas Smith, *The Works of Thomas Goodwin*, Vol. 4 (Reformation Heritage, 2006), p. 464.

were again the favourites, but once again had to settle for silver. When she retold the story of that Beijing final, even though I was fully aware of the outcome, I was desperate for her to win. It was somewhat heartbreaking to hear her describe the years of discipline, the training and the careful diet that goes into a tilt for Olympic gold—a tilt which was ultimately unsuccessful. Her crew also had to cope with the criticism of non-rowers back home who didn't seem to understand that, while not gold, an Olympic silver medal is still brilliant. Debbie is a Christian, and so I asked her the (somewhat leading) question, "Do you think you'll still regret the absence of Olympic gold when you get to heaven?"

Her response was clear:

> No, I won't take my rowing medals with me, and I think I'll be overwhelmed by joy when I'm there. It's how I live for Jesus that matters.

You can't take medals from this world with you into the new creation. But you can take a crown of glory—and it is a crown that never fades. Peter probably has in mind a contrast with crowns awarded at ancient sporting games. These were made of laurel leaves and flowers woven into olive branches, which looked good but would have barely lasted a week. The crown that awaits faithful shepherds, on the other hand, never fades. Lots of good things about ministry fade. We may enjoy the zeal of a new convert at church, but then sometimes that devotion fades a little with time. We may enjoy shoulder-to-shoulder partnership with some at church, but then sometimes they move elsewhere. We may enjoy a season when everything at church works and runs smoothly, but those seasons tend not to last.

But there is awaiting us a crown of glory that *never* fades. You know this, and I know this, but we need to *dwell* upon this. Let's heed Richard Baxter's advice:

> Bend thy soul to study eternity, busy thyself about the life to come, habituate thyself to such contemplations, and let not those thoughts be seldom and cursory, but bathe thy soul in heaven's delights; and if thy backward soul begins to flag ... call them back.[63]

Reward as a Motivation

I want to encourage you with the prospect of the "1 Peter 5:4 crown", which specifically awaits faithful pastors—and that's where we will get to at the end of this chapter. But it's helpful to set this particular truth in the wider context of how rewards function as a motivation in the New Testament. Sometimes we can be a little nervous here,[64] and it is right to highlight that a reward in glory is certainly not the only motivation for Christian living nor the only spur to faithful ministry. Yet, recurrently in the New Testament, rewards are held out as one reason to serve the Lord faithfully:[65]

---

63 Richard Baxter, *The Saints Everlasting Rest* (Benjamin Fawcett, 1811), p. 202. https://www.gutenberg.org/cache/epub/58135/pg58135-images.html (accessed 3 March 2026).

64 The strongest case against heavenly rewards that I've encountered is Craig Blomberg, "Degrees of Reward in the Kingdom of Heaven", *Journal of the Evangelical Theological Society* 35/2 (June 1992), p. 159-172.

65 Grant R. Osborne counts 28 times that the New Testament uses

For the Son of Man is going to come in his Father's glory with his angels, and then he will reward each person according to what they have done.
(Matthew 16:27)

[God] will repay each person according to what they have done. (Romans 2:6)

Since you call on a Father who judges each person's work impartially, live out your time as foreigners here in reverent fear. (1 Peter 1:17)

Then all the churches will know that I am he who searches hearts and minds, and I will repay each of you according to your deeds. (Revelation 2:23)

The time has come for judging the dead, and for rewarding your servants the prophets and your people who revere your name, both great and small.
(Revelation 11:18)

Then I heard a voice from heaven say, "Write this: blessed are the dead who die in the Lord from now on." "Yes," says the Spirit, "they will rest from their labour, for their deeds will follow them."
(Revelation 14:13)

Look, I am coming soon! My reward is with me, and I will give to each person according to what they have done. (Revelation 22:12)

---

the prospect of varying rewards as a motivation. See *Exegetical Commentary on the New Testament: Matthew* (Zondervan, 2010), p. 734.

That's just a selection, but enough to remind us that while every believer receives a crown for persevering to the end (1 Corinthians 9:25; 2 Timothy 4:8; James 1:12; Revelation 2:10), the Lord has promised varying rewards for believers, depending upon what they have done to serve him.

The criteria for God rewarding his people seem to be multiple:

- In the Sermon on the Mount, Jesus lists obedience to his teaching (Matthew 5:19), and he also stresses integrity; so a lack of hypocrisy in giving (6:4), and prayerfulness and fasting in private (v 6, 18) are rewarded.
- The parables of the minas and bags of gold stress making good use of the resources and opportunities we have been given to faithfully and ambitiously grow Christ's kingdom (Luke 19:11-27; Matthew 25:14-30).
- It seems that investing money in his kingdom can secure you a great reward of welcome (Luke 16:1-15).
- The quality of our work for the Lord will be tested and either rewarded or shown up as a waste (1 Corinthians 3:10-15).

So, we should be motivated by a future reward that varies depending upon what we have done—but we do need to be mindful of the danger that we begin to think that our labour for the Lord is heroic and deserves reward, so that we internally drift towards boasting in our labours. Maybe my own somewhat dutiful character needs to hear that more than you—but before we dwell upon the crown of glory, let's consider one striking reminder of God's bewildering grace.

What Will My Reward Be?

The parable of the vineyard workers in Matthew 20 is particularly helpful here. It reveals an extraordinarily generous God and warns against trying to calculate what our reward might be.

The context is Peter asking a question that I find echoed in my own heart sometimes: "We have left everything to follow you! What then will there be for us?" (Matthew 19:27). Notice Jesus doesn't rebuke Peter for this—rather, he gives two answers that offer a helpful balance. First he gives a phenomenal promise of reward:

> Truly I tell you, at the renewal of all things, when the Son of Man sits on his glorious throne, you who have followed me will also sit on twelve thrones, judging the twelve tribes of Israel. And everyone who has left houses or brothers or sisters or father or mother or wife or children or fields for my sake will receive a hundred times as much and will inherit eternal life. But many who are first will be last, and many who are last will be first. (v 28-30)

Yet then Jesus describes a landowner hiring workers for his vineyard. He hires some at 6 a.m. for the agreed salary of a denarius and then hires four other groups as the day goes on, the last group as late as 5 p.m.. It does not appear to be the fault of the last group that no one has hired them. I suppose it's probable that they are the least impressive physically. But regardless, clearly the "early morning workers" labour much harder than the "5 p.m.-ers". I suppose most of us would expect them to be paid very different wages. Yet that is not what happens:

> When evening came, the owner of the vineyard said to his foreman, "Call the workers and pay them their wages, beginning with the last ones hired and going on to the first." The workers who were hired about five in the afternoon came and each received a denarius. So when those came who were hired first, they expected to receive more. But each one of them also received a denarius. When they received it, they began to grumble against the landowner. "These who were hired last worked only one hour," they said, "and you have made them equal to us who have borne the burden of the work and the heat of the day."
>
> (20:8-12)

In this scene, the last are paid first (a reference back to 19:30). The shock of 20:9 is the generosity of the landowner. A denarius was a reasonable wage for 12 hours of work but a bizarrely kind one for one hour's work. No doubt the "5 p.m.-ers" were thrilled, but expectations were now raised for the "6 a.m.-ers"—only for them to receive the same wage. The substance of their complaint is very clear: "You have made them equal to us who have borne the burden of the work and heat of the day" (v 12).

For me, this is the genius of this parable—I sympathise with the grumbling of the "6 a.m.-ers". Do you not find your own sense of fairness offended by all of them receiving equal pay? Jesus wants to shock us a little. The narrative slows right down for the landowner's speech:

> I am not being unfair to you, friend. Didn't you agree to work for a denarius? Take your pay and go. I want to give the one who was hired last the same as I gave you. Don't I have the right to do what I want with my own money? Or are you envious because I am generous? (v 13-15)

The landowner has in no sense been unfair to his early worker, who received precisely what was promised. In any case, the landowner is free to do what he likes with his own money. The problem is that the 6 a.m. worker is envious (literally, "Is your eye evil?"). The early workers are questioning the landowner's generosity. This is an accusation against God.

The parable ends abruptly and without resolution. The effect is to leave the question hanging for you and me. Do we believe that God has the right to reward as he desires? Could we be envious of the reward that some have when we think we are more deserving? (As I write this, I personally feel undone.)

Then Jesus finishes with "So the last will be first, and the first will be last" (v 16).

This is surprising. Surely it should read, *The last will be the same as the first*, which is what happens in the parable. Yet Jesus has chosen to repeat 19:30 but reverses the clauses. (19:30 has first to last as primary, 20:16 has last to first.) It seems that 19:30 is an encouragement to the disciples—they may have nothing now but they will be rewarded. 20:16 is a caution to those same disciples against any kind of arrogant or presumptuous calculation of a reward.

Before we reach the great encouragement of the crown of glory, we need to have this frame in place. When it comes to future rewards, we must trust that the Lord is shockingly generous and be confident that no one is treated unfairly. It is unworthy and presumptuous for me to have any sense of calculating a reward. God's generosity and grace overwhelm our narrow opinions of what would be right. We must not reduce the wonderfully generous God down to our feeble system of calculations.

What Sort of Rewards?

The New Testament does not go into detail on the exact nature of rewards. Some texts suggest greater responsibility (Matthew 25:21, 23; Luke 19:17, 19). Other texts envisage praise from God (Matthew 25:21, 23; Luke 19:17; 1 Corinthians 4:5). Many writers have observed the importance of maintaining an organic connection between our labours now and our reward in the future. The future reward is not arbitrary. C.S. Lewis observed:

> Heaven offers nothing that a mercenary soul can desire. It is safe to tell the pure in heart that they shall see God, for only the pure in heart want to. There are rewards that do not sully motives. A man's love for a woman is not mercenary because he wants

> to marry her, nor his love for poetry mercenary because he wants to read it, nor his love of exercise less disinterested because he wants to run and leap and walk. Love, by definition, seeks to enjoy its object.[66]

I think it's possible to mount a case that when Jesus teaches, "Blessed are the pure in heart, for they will see God" (Matthew 5:8), it is meant to be the highpoint of the Beatitudes. All the others seem to have a connection between the first half and the second: the humble receive a kingdom; mourners receive comfort; the meek receive an inheritance; the hungry are filled; the merciful receive mercy. So it is natural to find a connection between purity of heart and seeing God. Those who desire God now will be rewarded with seeing him in glory. That is no surprise given the Old Testament background:

> The Lord bless you and keep you; the Lord make his face shine on you and be gracious to you; the Lord turn his face toward you and give you peace.
>
> (Numbers 6:24-26)

> One thing I ask from the Lord, this only do I seek: that I may dwell in the house of the Lord all the days of my life, to gaze upon the beauty of the Lord and to seek him in his temple. (Psalm 27:4)

> My heart says of you, "Seek his face!" Your face, Lord, I will seek. Do not hide your face from me, do not turn your servant away in anger. (Psalm 27:8-9)

---

66 C.S. Lewis, *The Problem of Pain* (HarperCollins, 2012), p. 149.

To see God's face is to receive his blessing. When God hides his face, it is a curse. Those who long to see God do so from the heart; they desire an undivided heart here and now. Isaiah offers a future where the great blessing is to see the Lord in his beauty. If you wholeheartedly serve the Lord now, you will see him clearly in the future. "Your eyes will see the king in his beauty and view a land that stretches afar" (Isaiah 33:17).

In the New Testament, seeing God remains our great hope. Currently we only have a shadowy glimpse of Jesus because just as you need pure eyes, without cataract or clouding, to see with clarity, so we need a pure heart, without division, to see God clearly:

> For now we see only a reflection as in a mirror; then we shall see face to face. Now I know in part; then I shall know fully, even as I am fully known.
> (1 Corinthians 13:12)

> And we all, who with unveiled faces contemplate the Lord's glory, are being transformed into his image with ever-increasing glory, which comes from the Lord, who is the Spirit. (2 Corinthians 3:18)

One day we will fully experience the beatific vision, seeing the Lord face to face:

> Dear friends, now we are children of God, and what we will be has not yet been made known. But we know that when Christ appears, we shall be like him, for we shall see him as he is. (1 John 3:2)

Not only is this a wonderful truth to dwell upon, but it helps us conceptualise the idea of believers receiving different rewards and yet still being blissfully happy. Anthony Hoeksema uses this illustration:

> When one has studied music and has attained some proficiency in playing a musical instrument, his capacity for enjoying music has been greatly increased. In a similar way, our devotion to Christ and to service in his kingdom increases our capacity for enjoying the blessing of that kingdom, both now and in the life to come.[67]

On a few occasions in the past, a friend who is a professional musician has given me some tickets for the Royal Opera House in London, where he works. I'm no great opera buff, but I still find it amazing: the sets, the voices, the intense atmosphere. On one such occasion, I took another friend who is a professionally trained musician, and they understood and appreciated it so much more! Their delight in the opera was much greater than mine because they had a greater capacity for musical enjoyment. What's more, their greater pleasure was somewhat infectious as they pointed out things I had not noticed. They dragged up my own capacity for joy.

Similarly, I am utterly confident that many others will have a greater reward in heaven than me because their service on earth was far greater. I am confident that they will have a richer experience of "seeing God" *and* that I will be blissfully happy. What's more, I take it that the new creation will not be static; we will continue to grow in delight, learning from the infectious joy

---

67 Anthony A. Hoeksema, *The Bible and the Future* (Eerdmans, 1979), p. 262.

of others. We look forward to an infinite unveiling, a journey deeper and deeper into the splendour of God, with each discovery brighter than the last. As Jonathan Edwards wrote:

> There shall be no such thing as envy in heaven, but perfect love shall reign through the whole society. Those who are not so high in glory as others, will not envy those that are higher, but will have so great and strong and pure love to them, that they will rejoice in their superior happiness. Their love to them will be such that they will rejoice that they are happier than themselves; so that instead of having a damp to their own happiness, it will add to it. They will see it to be fit that they that have been most eminent in works of righteousness should be the most highly exalted in glory.[68]

So it seems to me that, when it to comes to rewards in the new creation, we need to hold together two truths.

First, that our hope should be fixed upon seeing God. Nothing compares to that. I have loved this quote from Thomas Goodwin for many years:

> Let us therefore take God for our portion, whatsoever else becomes of us, whatsoever befalls us; let what will come, what afflictions, what throbs, what miseries or crosses will come, heaven will make amends for all; God will be better to thee than all.[69]

---

68 Jonathan Edwards, *The Portion of the Righteous (a sermon on Romans 2:10, December 1740)*, www.biblebb.com/files/edwards/portion2.htm (accessed 3 March 2026).

69 Ed. Thomas Smith, *The Works of Thomas Goodwin*, Vol. 4, p. 464.

When I'm at a low ebb, I repeat that simple phrase to myself:

> Heaven will make amends for all; God will be better to thee than all.

Maybe that is something you need to say to yourself or a friend right now. Similarly, Goodwin's fellow Puritan Thomas Watson expressed the same truth this way:

> One hour in heaven will make us forget all our sorrows! As the sun dries up the water, so one beam of God's glorious face will dry up all our tears.[70]

Brothers and sisters, keep going. You will be rewarded by seeing God. One beam will be enough. But we have all eternity.

Yet second, while the prospect of seeing God is extraordinary, the Lord knows our feeble hearts and so gives us a wide variety of images to encourage us. I find this observation of C.S. Lewis very helpful:

> The promise of Scripture may very roughly be reduced to five heads. It is promised (1) that we shall be with Christ; (2) that we shall be like Him; (3) with an enormous wealth of imagery, that we shall have "glory"; (4) that we shall, in some sense, be fed or feasted or entertained; and (5) that we shall have some sort of official position in the universe—ruling cities, judging angels, being pillars of God's temple. The first question I ask

---

70 Thomas Watson, *Meditation on Heaven,* quoted in Jennifer C. Watson, "Thomas Watson: The Necessity of Meditation" in Puritan Reformed Journal (2010), p. 166-181.

> about these promises is "Why any one of them except the first?" Can anything be added to the conception of being with Christ? ... The variation of the promises does not mean anything other than God will be our ultimate bliss; but because God is more than a Person, and lest we should imagine the joy of his presence too exclusively in terms of our present poor experience of personal love, with all its narrowness and strain and monotony, a dozen changing images, correcting and relieving each other are supplied.[71]

It will be better than we can possibly imagine. The Lord provides a rich variety of metaphors to begin to open our eyes to that. Again, I find Thomas Watson helpful in stimulating us to begin to comprehend the incomprehensible as he plays with the language of Revelation 21:

> What if all the dust of the earth were turned to silver; what if every stone were a wedge of gold; what if every flower were a ruby, every blade of grass a pearl, every grain of sand a diamond—yet what is all this, compared to Heaven? It is as impossible for any man to comprehend glory, as to "measure the heavens with a span," or drain the mighty ocean.[72]

---

71 C.S. Lewis, *The Weight of Glory and Other Addresses* (HarperCollins, 2001), p. 35.

72 Thomas Watson, *A Body of Divinity,* p64, https://www.monergism.com/thethreshold/sdg/watson/A Body of Divinity-Watson01.pdf (accessed 3 March 2026).

A Crown of Glory for Shepherds

So we are in a position to return to, and enjoy, Peter's promise: "When the Chief Shepherd appears, you will receive the crown of glory that will never fade away" (1 Peter 5:4).

What is striking is that this is a promise of a reward to "the elders among you" (v 1). While we would expect there to be echoes for all believers, this is a specifically targeted promise to shepherds. And as shepherds, we need to hear it. As we saw in the last chapter, there are trials that come upon pastors that are distinctive, or at least intensified, because they are engaged in the work of shepherding.

In 2 Timothy 2, Paul writes to his "son" Timothy, telling him: "The things you have heard me say in the presence of many witnesses entrust to reliable people who will also be qualified to teach others. Join with me in suffering like a good soldier of Christ Jesus" (v 1-3). In *that* context, of training others to be shepherds and the cost that comes of standing firm for Jesus as a shepherd, Paul writes:

> Anyone who competes as an athlete does not receive the victor's crown except by competing according to the rules. (v 5)

The "rules" in the context of 2 Timothy are that a faithful teaching ministry brings suffering. It seems reasonable to assume that this, then, is the crown of 1 Peter 5:4: a reward for the faithful endurance of suffering in the service of Jesus, particularly in the work of teaching, evangelising and training up others for the same work.

But what *is* this crown? Paul refers to a crown in two other places with a deeply personal application:

> Therefore, my brothers and sisters, you whom I love and long for, my joy and crown, stand firm in the Lord in this way, my dear friends. (Philippians 4:1)

> For what is our hope, our joy, or the crown in which we will glory in the presence of our Lord Jesus when he comes? Is it not you? (1 Thessalonians 2:19)

Paul's crown and joy (perhaps we could say, his crowning joy) is those who have been converted under his ministry. He anticipates a reward for shepherding them, and, again, there is an organic connection between his labour and his reward. There is a sense that in the new creation, part of Paul's reward is enjoyment of these believers. Jonathan Edwards observed:

> Christ and his disciples, while on earth, were often together in affliction and trial, and they kept up and manifested the strongest love and friendship to each other under great and sore sufferings. And now in heaven they enjoy each other's love in immortal glory, all sorrow and sighing having forever fled away.[73]

As a pastor, you have the enormous privilege of walking through many different seasons of life with your flock here on earth. It creates deep bonds of affection, which will be deeper and richer still in the new creation. Paul dreams for that day, when he sees those he ministered

73 Jonathan Edwards, "Heaven a Place of Love" in *Charity and Its Fruits* (Banner of Truth, 1998 reprint), p. 343.

to standing in glory. Those are the gold medals that will last for ever. Every worldly achievement will fade to nothing, but in those you have pastored, you have a legacy that will last into eternity.

I had a brief hint of this recently when my wife and I visited some mission partners that our church sent out a few years ago to work in a theological college in East Africa. They asked me to give a few lectures while there and at the start introduced me in a manner that made me well up with tears: "This is Matt, who was our pastor for 18 years. He taught us the faith, saw us get married, buried one of our children and baptised the other two. We're here because of his encouragement. Enjoy the lecture."

I can't remember feeling quite so acutely, "Here are people I love—my joy and my crown".

I encourage you to pause right now and think about those whom you have seen come to Christ as a result of your ministry and those whom you have seen strengthened in Christ, endure hardship and serve others, due, in some part, to your ministry.

Can you imagine standing around the throne of the Lamb in the new creation, praising him together and smiling at each other as you enjoy your glorious Saviour? Don't rush away from that picture. Dwell upon it. Elaborate it. Enjoy it.

Yes—an unfading crown of glory awaits you.

Chapter 8

Sowing by Faith

Richard Johnson was the first chaplain to New South Wales in Australia. With the encouragement of John Newton and William Wilberforce, he was appointed to sail with the first fleet of British ships that established Australia as a prison colony in 1788. Responsible for the spiritual life of those first 1,400 settlers and the education of the convicts, Johnson had to endure humiliation at the hands of Francis Grose, the senior administrator of the colony. Grose allowed Johnson to hold only one service on a Sunday, from 6:00-6:45 a.m.—and when Johnson asked for a church building, Grose dismissively replied that "a sentry box was at [his] service".

That is not an encouraging start to your ministry! And it didn't get much better—from there, church-service attendance dwindled. And yet John Newton wrote this to Johnson in 1791:

> I have not been disheartened by your apparent want of success. I have been told that skilful gardeners

> will sow and raise a salad for dinner in the short time while the meat is roasting. But no gardener can raise oaks with such expedition. You are sent to New Holland [Australia] not to sow salad seeds, but to plant acorns, and your labours will not be lost, though the first appearance may be very small and the progress very slow. You are, I trust, planting for the next century. I have good hope that your oaks will spring up and flourish and spread among the islands and nations of the southern seas.[74]

I was shown that quote by Peter Jensen, former Archbishop of Sydney, while we sat in the library of Moore College. That theological college in Sydney currently has more than 300 students, who graduate to serve the Lord in Australia and all over the world. The diocese of Sydney alone now has roughly 400 evangelical churches.

Those are fine oak trees that have sprung up, flourished and spread!

As I read Newton's letter, I had a picture of him chatting to his friend Richard Johnson as they rest in heaven awaiting the new creation. Newton is smiling as he says to Johnson, "See, I was right! Although, to be honest, even I didn't envisage the Lord producing quite so many fine oaks. The seed you sowed more than 200 years ago has borne a fruit beyond all we could ask or imagine."

---

74 Quoted in Stuart Piggin and Robert Linder, *The Fountain of Public Prosperity: Evangelical Christians in Australian History 1740-1914* (Monash University Publishing, 2018), p. 82. I am grateful to Peter Jensen for sharing this with me.

Who of us has not, at times, been disheartened by lack of success in ministry?

But... maybe we are planting for the next century!

Not long after I had been converted, I went to a prayer meeting where a man was visiting who was back on home assignment from the mission field in Pakistan. I asked him, "So, have you seen much fruit from your labours?" (I was very pleased with myself for having quickly learned the appropriate "Christianese language".) The man paused and then said:

> No, we haven't seen much fruit in terms of conversions. There are times when I wonder if we have sown a great deal of seed or barely any. Yet, to push the metaphor, sometimes it feels as though we're removing stones from the field for the next generation to plant and later generations to harvest. Maybe the Lord will allow us to see fruit in our generation, but I know it will come at some point.[75]

I know it will come at some point. I have often reflected on that saint's perseverance and confidence in the face of little evidence of growth. That was faith.

An Expectant Hope

Where did this man's hope come from? How was Newton able to encourage Johnson with such clear confidence?

---

75 To my shame, I cannot remember the man's name. But if you are the guy who came from Pakistan to visit Birmingham University Christian Union in 1993 and endured the clumsy questions of a new convert, then I look forward to thanking you in glory.

Presumably it was because they believed what Jesus taught about growing seed:

> He ... said, "This is what the kingdom of God is like. A man scatters seed on the ground. Night and day, whether he sleeps or gets up, the seed sprouts and grows, though he does not know how. All by itself the soil produces grain—first the stalk, then the head, then the full kernel in the head. As soon as the grain is ripe, he puts the sickle to it, because the harvest has come." (Mark 4:26-29)

It may take a long time, but where the word of God is sown, the kingdom of Jesus will grow.

It's a wonderfully heartening picture that Jesus gives. I particularly love the words in the middle: "The seed sprouts and grows, *though he does not know how*". There's not a lot of detail there—maybe the farmer is inexperienced and really doesn't understand how grain grows, or maybe the ground that he is trying to grow in is terribly inhospitable. But there is growth, and there is growth because he sowed, and then things happened that he was unaware of and could not completely explain. We can't see the growth under the ground. We don't know if there is something significant happening. We don't know when we will see the fruit—or if it will show itself after our time. But we trust by faith that seed will grow. Where the word of God is sown, the kingdom of God will grow!

You and I know this. But you and I need to *know* this. We need to believe it as we get out of bed, as we start work, as we pray, as we preach, as we counsel, as we plan, as we work late, as we sleep, and as we get up and go again. Where the word of God is sown, the kingdom of Jesus will grow—including in the corner of his world and in the parcel of time where Jesus has granted you the privilege of sowing his seed.

I want to take you to four short illustrations that give us a glimpse of the truth of Jesus' parable in reality. Maybe pick the one or two that most resonate with and encourage you, and remember them, repeat them to yourself from time to time, and believe the truth they portray.

1. Worldwide Data

In 1910, there were approximately 600 million Christians in the world. By 2010 there were about 2.2 billion. Estimates are that by 2050 the number will be 3.3 billion.[76] Now think back to the size of the kingdom when Jesus uttered those words in Mark 4. There were at most a few dozen people who were its members. So what do you think those first twelve disciples thought and envisaged when Jesus taught them about sowing seed? Did they really believe that what began with themselves, a bunch of uneducated fishermen with the odd ex-tax-collector and reformed Zealot thrown in, could become a kingdom encompassing about a third of the global population within a couple of millennia?

---

76 These are obviously difficult numbers to be certain about. Only God counts his sheep accurately! But, see https://www.pewresearch.org/religion/2011/12/19/new-pew-forum-study-estimates-global-christian-population-at-2-18-billion/?utm_source=chatgpt.com, and https://goodfaithmedia.org/global-christian-population-projected-to-reach-3-3-billion-by-2050/?utm_source=chatgpt.com (accessed 3 March 2026).

2. Martin Luther

Reading Mark 4 makes me think of Martin Luther's timeless sermon:

> I opposed indulgences and all the papists, but never with force. I simply taught, preached and wrote God's word; otherwise I did nothing. And while I slept or drank Wittenberg beer with my friends Philip and Amsdorf, the word so greatly weakened the papacy that no prince or emperor ever inflicted such losses upon it. I did nothing; I let the word do its work.[77]

3. China

When it comes to unseen growth, there's not much more encouraging to consider than the Chinese church. When all foreign missionaries were forced to leave the country in 1953, the church was estimated to consist of about 700,000 people. Imagine being one of those missionaries, forced to leave the field you'd been called to, with no idea of what was going on. For years, very little news leaked out of China. And yet the word of God had been planted, so that despite the lack of foreign support, the church grew to today's figure of somewhere between 70 and 100 million—perhaps about 7% of the population.[78]

---

77 https://wittenbergcenter.de/martin-luther-and-the-beer?utm_source=chatgpt.com (accessed 3 March 2026).

78 https://www.pewresearch.org/religion/2023/08/30/christianity/?utm_source=chatgpt.com (accessed 3 March 2026).

4. The Faithful Plodder

One personal hero for me is William Carey.[79] Partly it's because he described himself as a "faithful plodder", and I can relate to that. In part, I'm impressed by the fact that he undertook the four-month voyage to India when he was told it was a stupid thing to do; he trusted God and thought otherwise. Carey arrived in 1793, and until 1800 *he did not see a single convert.* Carey was preaching up to three or four times day during this season and was stoned on a few occasions. I can imagine that after seven years of no one coming to faith, you might start to question whether this was the right ministry. But Carey kept going.

When his son moved to plant a new church in another part of the country, Carey wrote to him:

> We have the greatest encouragement to go forward in the work of our Lord Jesus, because we have every reason to conclude that it will be successful at last. It is the cause which God has had in his mind from eternity, the cause for which Christ shed his blood, that for which the Spirit and word of God were given ... The success thereof is therefore certain. Be encouraged, therefore, my dear son, to devote yourself entirely to it, and to pursue it as a matter of the very first importance even to your dying day.[80]

---

79 As a legacy-leaver, not as a husband, as some have noted; https://christianhistoryinstitute.org/magazine/article/william-careys-less-than-perfect-family-life (accessed 3 March 2026).

80 https://www.gutenberg.org/cache/epub/2056/pg2056-images.html?utm_source=chatgpt.com (accessed 3 March 2026).

By the end of his life, Carey had translated the New Testament into 35 dialects and languages. Today it is estimated that there are 72 million believers in India or 4.9% of the population—and this despite significant persecution. In Newton's language, those are fine oak trees that grew from an inauspicious beginning.

What Results Will We See in Glory?

Have you heard of John Warr? Neither had I. He was an apprentice shoemaker who worked alongside William Carey, and he was the first person to share the gospel with him. Carey didn't become a Christian until a few years afterwards, but it was John Warr who first made him take the claims of Jesus seriously. One small seed of the word of God was planted as they made shoes together—and that seed has grown into a lot of oaks.

I like to think of John Warr meeting Richard Johnson in heaven and them chuckling together about what became of their apparently small seed-sowing. And maybe you will chuckle with them one day—because who knows the particular outcome of the seeds that you have sown? How many conversations will you and I end up having like that? How many times will we discover that we have been one small link in a chain that was amazing?

When I was a schoolteacher, once a year I would run a short evangelistic course during the lunch break. Typically, between four and eight unbelieving pupils would come along. In the final school where I taught, after a few years I was permitted to organise an "events week", with external Christian speakers coming in each day to share the gospel. I poured myself into this, and somewhere around 100 pupils came over the course of the week.

But I didn't see a single pupil become a Christian.

Not one.

When I left teaching to work for a church, I was distressed that I hadn't seen any conversions among the pupils in my time as a teacher.

Then, two months after I had finished teaching, I went and spoke at a university outreach event organised by the Christian Union. Afterwards, a student came up to me. I had taught him at school. "Hello, sir," he said. "I thought you would like to know that I couldn't get those lunchtimes when we talked about Jesus out of my head. I spent the summer reading the New Testament and so when I arrived here at uni and saw an advert for the Christian Union, I thought I would go along. I became a Christian the first night that I went."

Amazing. I have always thought that this was a profound kindness of the Lord to me personally. I learned in experience what I know to be true biblically: you sow the seed of the word of God but don't always get to see the results.

Similarly, on a few occasions I've had kind emails from pastors in churches in other cities in the UK or further afield, telling me that "non-Christian so-and-so", who had sat in our church services for a few months while they lived in London before moving away, had become a Christian further down the line, and that clearly the truths they had heard while in London were used by God's Spirit to bring conviction. I am very grateful that these pastors troubled to write. Sometimes, we do not see the results, but we sow in faith. And sometimes, the Lord is kind enough to let us know what happened with one of the seeds. I suspect that you will spend quite a while in the new creation discovering what happened with many of the others, especially those seeds that you sowed when you felt tired or weak or discouraged, but you sowed them anyway.

Sowing for the Next Generation

Newton's perspective was that sometimes we are sowing for the next century or at least the next generation. It was one shared by no less a servant of God than King David. By the end of his reign, he knew that he would not build the temple in Jerusalem—but look at his generosity in making good plans for the one who would, his son Solomon:

> King David rose to his feet and said: "Listen to me, my fellow Israelites, my people. I had it in my heart to build a house as a place of rest for the ark of the covenant of the LORD, for the footstool of our God, and I made plans to build it. But God said to me, 'You are not to build a house for my Name, because you are a warrior and have shed blood' ... He said to me, 'Solomon your son is the one who will build my house and my courts, for I have chosen him to be my son, and I will be his father' ...
>
> "My son Solomon, the one whom God has chosen, is young and inexperienced. The task is great, because

> this palatial structure is not for man but for the LORD God. With all my resources I have provided for the temple of my God—gold for the gold work, silver for the silver, bronze for the bronze, iron for the iron and wood for the wood, as well as onyx for the settings, turquoise, stones of various colours, and all kinds of fine stone and marble—all of these in large quantities. Besides, in my devotion to the temple of my God I now give my personal treasures of gold and silver for the temple of my God, over and above everything I have provided for this holy temple."
>
> (1 Chronicles 28:2-3, 6; 29:1-3)

David's ministry ambition was to build the temple in Jerusalem, but God said no. It was a task for the next generation. There was no frustration expressed by David and no resentment. Rather he worked hard to gather from the people the resources to build the temple, and he gave sacrificially himself—all for the cause of a temple he would not live to see. His approach was, *The Lord must be honoured with a temple. I will not achieve that in my lifetime, but I am going to do everything within my power to ensure that it happens after me.* There is something wonderful in that. Clearly David had a mixed record when it came to his faithfulness to God, but on this point he finished well.

Mike Ovey was one of my lecturers when I was at Oak Hill Theological College, and he went on to be the principal. He was an outstanding scholar and fine leader, who died suddenly and tragically in his fifties. But he left a significant legacy. He often expressed to his students the desire that they would be better than the generation before: that they would go further. At the end of one ordination service, he said:

> We want you to be better than us, we want you to be more faithful than us—we want you, spiritually speaking, to tower above us so that the cross of the Lord Jesus Christ stands high in this land and that men and women may know the blessings of eternal life. That is our dream for you, that is our prayer for you, not that you are as we are, but that you are better.[81]

He was a brilliant man but had very little ego. He cared about the growth of Christ's kingdom and was content to sow seed in the hope that the harvest would be more obvious in later generations. He believed Mark 4. It was a wonderful ambition.

Most of us in ministry are familiar with the task of passing on the baton to the next generation, following the pattern that Paul gave Timothy:

> The things you have heard me say in the presence of many witnesses entrust to reliable people who will also be qualified to teach others. (2 Timothy 2:2)

Often it seems very routine and unimpressive. It is simply sharing life and ministry, the joys and struggles, with someone a few years younger. Yet it is wonderfully fruit-bearing! I recently received this text from a pastor who had been with us as a student and then for a few years as a young professional before heading into ministry:

---

81 https://credomag.com/2017/01/mike-oveys-pastoral-wisdom-for-future-ministers-of-the-gospel/ (accessed 3 March, 2026).

> Hi Matt. I started a preaching group at our house with six younger guys going through 2 Timothy. Very fond memories of doing the same thing with you 15 years ago. It was so formative. Keep going, our labours are not in vain.

That message popped up on my phone on a bad day in a bad week in a low month in a difficult year! It was priceless. I badly needed to know in that season that our labours in the Lord are not in vain!

Not of all of us will have the long-term impact of a Richard Johnson or William Carey, but there will undoubtedly be fruit that we cannot see now but that we will be delighted by when we realise our contribution in glory. The Lord will use our labours to achieve immeasurably more than we ask or imagine. That is his way (Ephesians 3:20).

So, brothers and sisters, keep sowing in faith. Where the word of God is sown, the kingdom of Jesus will grow. It may be unseen by us farmers. We may never see oak trees rise up in our lifetimes. But we can be certain that there is fruit. God promises that it is so.

Chapter 9

Manna Every Day

You'll have picked up by now that I think that a regular dose of John Newton will do any minister the world of good. One letter that I turn back to frequently is titled, "What are the most obvious causes, symptoms and effects of a decline in the spiritual life?"[82]

Newton's three top causes are striking. First is heretical error. That could take many forms and is beyond the scope of this book. The other two are "spiritual pride and self-complacence" and "an inordinate desire and attachment to the things of the present world". In other words, assuming that you're being faithful to the Scriptures, Newton thinks the two things that will most hurt your spiritual life and rob you of your joy in pastoring are, first, pride and, second, worldliness.

It is not surprising that if we are self-satisfied, then we will not demonstrate a suitable reliance upon the Lord. Newton has a particular warning for those who are gifted:

---

82 John Newton, *The Works of John Newton,* Vol. 4, p. 602.

> Ministers who are honoured with singular abilities and success have great need of watchfulness and prayer on this account ... perhaps the poor worm is secretly indulging self-applause and pleasing himself with the numbers and attention of those who hang upon his words.[83]

Let's not be those who experience growing ministries and yet become poor worms!

And let's be killing sin before it grows. It becomes far easier to justify "mild sin" when we're exhausted, discouraged and self-pitying. There can be a little voice in our heads which says, "Poor me; life is currently hard and disappointing. I think I deserve another drink; I deserve a little attention from that woman; it's okay to watch that stuff online." Newton observes:

> The practice of a single sin, or the omission of a single duty, if allowed against the light of conscience, and if habitual, will be sufficient to keep the soul weak, unfruitful and uncomfortable and lay it open to the impression of every surrounding temptation.[84]

In other words: don't listen to the voice of self-pity!

When it comes to the second joy-robber—loving the things of this world too much—I think it is perhaps easier to avoid when we start in ministry than as we go on in it. I've observed (in my own heart, and others have said the same) that as the years go by and non-ministry peers do well in their careers, envy sparked by our current finances or anxiety about our future finances can begin

83 As above, p. 604.
84 As above, p. 606.

to grow. It is possible to become quite entitled as the years go by. It's a real danger, and we are perhaps wise to strive to lean towards frugality. Newton would warn us:

> Unless this evil principle be mortified in its root, by the doctrine of the cross, it will in time prevail over the most splendid profession.[85]

Think of Judas:

> But one of his disciples, Judas Iscariot, who was later to betray him, objected, "Why wasn't this perfume sold and the money given to the poor? It was worth a year's wages." He did not say this because he cared about the poor but because he was a thief; as keeper of the money bag, he used to help himself to what was put into it. (John 12:4-6)

Or let me mention, again, Demas, once a "fellow worker" of Paul's but no longer—why?

> Demas, because he loved this world, has deserted me. (2 Timothy 4:10)

Once again, we must remember what we have:

> In a word, you are not poor but rich. The promises are your inheritance; heaven is your home; the angels are ministering spirits who rejoice to watch over you for your good; and the Lord of angels himself is your sun and shield, and everlasting portion. It is impossible that you, to whom he has given himself, his Son, his Spirit, his grace, his kingdom, can want

85 As above, p. 605.

> anything that it truly good for you. If riches were so, he could pour them upon you in abundance, as easily as he provides you your daily bread.[86]

So, the joyful pastor will be seeking *not* to do two things: not to allow spiritual pride to take root or love of the things of this world to grow. But, above all, he will be seeking to do one thing above all. The pastor who is (despite everything) joyful will be the pastor who treasures Christ.

I know that there have been times when I have felt deeply jaded and weary and was serving without joy. And I can point to seasons and circumstances and, yes, other people that have contributed to that joylessness. But sometimes, and probably more often than I like to admit, it is really my fault. I've simply not spent enough time with Jesus. I've neglected the one thing that I need above all else. I imagine that this happens because I don't want to be weak and needy. I want a stockpile of wisdom and strength that means I can be self-reliant. I don't want to have to trust every day for manna. Yes, there are times when I simply need more rest. There are times when I need someone to show me a practical solution. There are seasons when I need friends to speak truth to me. But mostly I simply need to remember some basic truth that we saw set out so powerfully by John Owen back in chapter 4:

> Do any of us find decays in grace prevailing in us; deadness, coldness, lukewarmness, a kind of spiritual stupidity and senselessness coming upon us? ... Let

86 John Newton, *The Works of John Newton,* Vol. 1, p. 206.

> us assure ourselves there is no better way for our healing and deliverance, yea, no other way but this alone, namely, the obtaining a fresh view of the glory of Christ by faith, and a steady abiding therein. Constant contemplation of Christ and his glory, putting forth its transforming power unto the revival of all grace, is the only relief in this case.[87]

I need manna every day. I need to contemplate Christ every day. That is the way to remain joyful, not jaded. It is a simple thing—but it has taken me decades of ministry to learn. When I need healing and deliverance—when I am feeling cold or lukewarm—what I need, and all I need, is "a fresh view of the glory of Christ". And so do you.

I think that more than anyone else, it is John Newton who has encouraged me to find the joy in ministry and not just dwell upon the sorrows. He has spurred me to dwell upon the sweet and not the bitter. I hope this book has done that for you—but I want to give the final word to him:

> A comfortable freedom for public service depends much upon the spirituality of our walk before God and man. Wisdom will not dwell with a trifling, an assuming, a censorious, or a worldly spirit. But if it is our business to contemplate Jesus, and to walk in his steps, he will bless us, we shall be like trees planted by streams of water , and he will bless the work of our hands.[88]

---

87 Ed. William H. Goold, *The Glory of Christ: The Works of John Owen,* Vol. 1 (Banner of Truth, 1965), p. 395.

88 John Newton, *The Works of John Newton,* Vol. 1, p. 96.

thegoodbook COMPANY

BIBLICAL | RELEVANT | ACCESSIBLE

At The Good Book Company we are dedicated to helping Christians and local churches grow. We believe that God's growth process always starts with hearing clearly what he has said to us through his timeless and flawless word—the Bible.

Ever since we opened our doors in 1991, we have been striving to produce resources that are biblical, relevant, and accessible. By God's grace, we have grown to become an international publisher, encouraging ordinary Christians of every age and stage and every background and denomination to live for Christ day by day and equipping churches to grow in their knowledge of God, their love for one another, and the effectiveness of their outreach.

Call one of our friendly team for a discussion of your needs or visit one of our local websites for more information on the resources and services we provide.

Your friends at The Good Book Company

thegoodbook.com | thegoodbook.co.uk
thegoodbook.com.au | thegoodbook.co.nz